GUIDEPOSTS

An Angel's Touch

An Angel's Touch

*True Stories about Angels, Miracles
and Answers to Prayer*

NATHALIE LADNER-BISCHOFF

CARMEL, NEW YORK 10512

www.guidepostsbooks.com

This Guideposts edition is published by special arrangement with Pacific Press Publishing Association.

Edited by Glen Robinson

Ladner-Bischoff, Nathalie, 1931-
An angel's touch: true stories about angels,
miracles, and answers to prayers/Nathalie Ladner-Bischoff.
p. cm.
ISBN 0-8163-1577-9 (pbk. : alk. paper)
1. Angels. I. Title.
BT966.2.L23   1998
235'.3—dc21   97-41473
CIP

www.guidepostsbooks.com
Jacket and interior design by José R. Fonfrias
Typeset by Composition Technologies, Inc.
Cover photo by Scala/Art Resource, NY

PRINTED IN THE UNITED STATES OF AMERICA

*To my precious, number-one critiquer, best friend
and husband, Marvin,
who patiently spent many hours alone
while I wrote and revised
the contents of this book.
Thank you, Marvin!
You make my life worthwhile.*

Contents

Contents

Acknowledgments

THERE ARE MANY PEOPLE who helped me put together this compilation of stories about angels, miracles, and answers to prayer. I would like to acknowledge a few of them:

Gratefully, I am indebted to my friend and well-known author, the late Vera Lee Wiggins, for selling her computer to me and going the second mile to teach me computer techniques and expedite the completion of this book.

I am also grateful to Bruce Toews for the valuable time he spent moving, setting up, and programming my computer. Thank you, Bruce, for your ongoing instruction and expertise.

To members of our local Christian Scribes Club for their helpful critiques and suggestions, I offer my sincere "Thank you!"

Above all, I am grateful to all my Christian friends who willingly shared their true, exciting, faith-boosting stories necessary for composing this book. Undoubtedly it will inspire readers' faith in our ever-loving, ever-caring heavenly Father. Praise Him for His continual goodness to the children of earth!

An Angel's Touch

Who Was That Man?

I N EARLY MARCH, my husband, Wilmer, and I drove to Spokane to tend to our ranch business. The lush fields of winter wheat shimmered in the sun's warmth. The seventy miles north of our small town passed by quickly. After we completed our errands and left town, we noticed dark clouds jostling one another in the western sky.

At dusk we left the boarding academy where we'd stopped to visit our son. About thirty miles from home, Wilmer said, "Looks like we've had heavy rain."

"It must have been a downpour! Just look at all the mud the water washed onto the road!" I exclaimed.

Near St. John, a small town fifteen miles from home, we found more mud on the road. At the next bend, a barricade stood across the road with a sign that read: "Road Closed. Water Over Road."

"Now what are we going to do?" I asked. "Go around through Winona?" Winona, a small town, was twenty miles farther from home. "Let's go by your friend Speedy's place and see what he thinks."

"Okay, I'll see what Speedy says," Wilmer agreed.

"I wouldn't advise you to go around the barricade, Wilmer," Speedy advised. "Late this afternoon and evening we had a heavy cloudburst. The road is washed out in places. A lot of mud washed onto the road from the fields. You'd best go around the detour through Winona."

As we backed out of Speedy's driveway, my husband said, "I'm going to try it. I don't think it can be that bad."

"I wish you wouldn't try it. Let's follow the detour through Winona," I said.

"We've only ten miles to go this way. Just don't worry about it," my husband insisted, and drove around the barricade. The mud became deeper and thicker. Our car wallowed through the mud, around a sharp bend and down the half-mile grade. Beyond our headlights, thick darkness awaited us.

Near the bottom of the grade, our headlights revealed a large expanse of debris—a hundred-foot-long stretch of mud, small and large rocks—with no roadway in sight!

We stopped. We could have backed up the grade, I imagine. But Wilmer climbed out of the car, "I'm going to walk across this mud and see how bad it really is!"

"Oh, Lord," I pleaded. "We've been foolish. We had no business going around the barricade. Now we're here. Please help us, Lord."

With mud coating his shoes and pant legs, my husband climbed into the car. "I'm going to try crossing it. I think we can make it."

I took a big breath and said, "Oh, no!" Wilmer drove ahead. Bounce, bounce, bounce our car lurched forward. There was another bounce and a thud—and we landed on a big rock and held fast. With one front wheel in the air, the other buried in the mud, we sat there wondering what to do.

Two months prior, Wilmer had had open-heart surgery and was told not to lift anything heavy. He would take his life in his hands if he tried to dig the rock out from under the car. Besides, we didn't have a shovel.

I prayed earnestly, "Lord, please forgive us. If you possibly can, and see fit, please help us out of this predicament."

The entire length of the roadway lay straight behind us, but we didn't see lights approaching. Suddenly a pickup was there. Headlights beamed through our rear window. A man got out and came toward our car. My husband opened the door.

"Are you in trouble?" the man asked.

Wilmer explained what we had done. The man didn't say another word. He went to his truck, got a shovel, came back and began digging the mud away from under the big rock that kept our front wheel suspended. After he removed enough mud and pulled the rock from under it, the car again rested on the ground.

"I think we can make it now," Wilmer told him. "We're over the worst of it already. Thanks a million for your help."

As Wilmer crawled into the car, I asked, "Who was that man?"

My husband, born and raised in that area, knew everyone living on the farms and in the towns. "I've never seen him before. I don't even recognize the pickup." He shut the door. We turned to wave, but there was no man! No pickup! Nothing!

He couldn't have backed up the grade because we would have seen his receding headlights. There was no room on the debris-covered road for him to pass us; we would have had to go first. I said, "Thank You, Lord! You never fail us when we're in trouble."

As told by Myrna Lighthouse.

CHAPTER 2

He's Listening

FTER MY HUSBAND DIED, I had only God to help me do our ranch business. He had a double indemnity life insurance policy, and due to his accidental death it was a large sum. It was something to help me operate our ranch for a few years.

My lawyer went through the large estate and prepared many papers. Due to the size of the estate, it had to be submitted not only to the state, but also to the federal government. After the lawyer submitted all of his papers to these two agencies, he told me, "If the federal government accepts it, then the state probably will too, and we'll be all right." The federal government accepted, but Washington state did not. The state delayed proceedings.

My lawyer told me, "Mryna, if the state government turns it down, then the federal government is going to say, 'We must have missed something. We're going to have to review the estate papers once more.'"

If this happened, it might take almost all of the insurance money I'd received to pay the estate taxes. After I learned this, I worried and worried, and prayed and prayed. At night, I prayed, "Lord, I don't know what to do. You're just going to have to take care of this." The next morning, I'd pick up that worry and carry it with me all day. I would worry. I would cry. I'd worry and pray continually.

One Sabbath, when I went to church, I don't remember the pastor's sermon topic, but I remember him saying, "You're not doing what the Lord wants you to do. You are not letting the Lord have this problem. You insist on carrying it around every day. Get rid of it." All the way home from church, I cried and prayed, "Lord, I've had it! I'm through worrying. I can't handle this worry any more. You take it from here, and whatever You do will be all right with me." After that I had more peace than I'd had since my husband died.

As usual, on the way home from church, I picked up the mail. After I got home, I thumbed through it. I discovered a letter from my lawyer. As a rule, I never open the mail on Sabbath unless it's a personal letter. I thought, "I'm going to see what he says."

I opened that letter and read: "Mryna, it's all done. The state has decided to settle."

That wasn't all. When you settle an estate, you send a check with it. This shows the government that you're paying your estate taxes. Then if they accept it, fine. I had sent my check for the estate taxes. The government returned the check to me. The estate settlement cost me only my lawyer's fee. You see, God had something much better for me when I let Him have my problem. He knew beforehand that I would commit the entire problem to Him. The Lord is very special to me. He's constantly showing me that He's listening! He hasn't always said, "Yes," but He lets me know He's listening! Always!

As told by Myrna Lighthouse.

5

Warm Angel Hands

HUNDER ROARED, threatening a monsoon downpour on the island of Borneo. Repeatedly, lightning flashed. Black clouds tumbled and jostled across the mountain village as six-year-old Adek and his eight-year-old sister Noni raced across the swinging footbridge to attend the five o'clock Vacation Bible School.

"Hurry, Adek! We'll get soaked before we get to church," Noni called over her shoulder as big raindrops pelted them.

"I am hurrying," Adek said. He carefully hung onto the guidewire of the bridge and followed Noni across the twenty-foot deep gully that separated their home from the Kiulu church.

In the foothills of Mt. Kinabalu, over 14,550 feet high, the church is surrounded by coconut groves, which shade the bamboo huts or mahogany-board homes. These village homes are nestled on both sides of the gully next to the church. The gully stream, a tributary of the Tuaran River, held hungry crocodiles.

To make the swinging bridge, the villagers anchored four sixty-foot steel cables to trees on either side of the gully. To the cables they fastened wire or rope and wove thin mahogany boards through the wires to form the swinging footbridge. This bridge connected the gully-divided village.

The children raced to church. Their little pet dogs followed, to crawl under the church's bamboo floor. As the children sang "Jesus Loves Me," the dogs howled to complete the choir.

While they sang, rain pounded the tin roof into a deafening roar. The teachers quit talking. They stopped singing. The children grew frightened and restless. They all knew that within fifteen minutes four inches of water would cover the ground.

During the ferocious cloudburst, one of the deacons ran to check the gully. He raced back to the church shouting, "Dismiss the children at once. They must cross the bridge before it's covered with water!"

"Run quickly!" the deacon shouted. Drenched children who lived on the other side of the gully dashed across the bridge safely, all except Adek and Noni.

"Hang on to your brother!" the deacon shouted to Noni. Now waist-deep in water, Noni neared the other end of the bridge. She hung onto the wire with one hand and grabbed her brother's hand with the other, when suddenly a wall of water rushed over them and wrenched Adek from her grasp. The torrent swept both children off the bridge.

"Adek's gone!" Noni yelled. She grabbed a tree root and tenaciously clung to it. Nearby friends pulled her from the seething water. Like a cork, Adek bobbed as he drifted downstream. The men ran along the bank, afraid Adek would be bashed against rocks or logs. They held out a stick to Adek, but angry water ripped him quickly away. At a sharp bend in the gully, a current pulled him underwater.

"Send men down to the river," the deacon shouted as daylight darkened. Using torches and flashlights, the men patrolled the river, hoping and praying they'd find Adek before a hungry crocodile did. All night they searched and couldn't find Adek. Meanwhile at the church, the pastor held an all-night prayer vigil with the teachers and mothers.

At sunrise, one of the searchers spotted Adek, soaked and shivering, leaning against a tree. He rushed to grab him, hugged him close and shouted, "Adek's saved! I've found him!" The men hastily carried Adek to church where they wrapped him in blankets.

"Tell us how you got out of that swirling water! Without help it was impossible for you to get out of the gully. We searched for you all night. What happened?" They all talked at once.

"The water pushed me along very fast, but suddenly a log stopped me and held me. Then I told myself, 'I'm going to die.' Next, I felt strong, warm hands grab my body and pull me away from the log. Then I found myself under that tree."

Adek's mother cuddled him close. Her swollen eyes filled with tears of joy. After she warmed Adek, she joined her family and church members in a joyous praise service thanking God for saving her son.

After the praise service, Adek's father told the group, "My wife and I didn't believe in God before this happened. Now we know that there is a God in Heaven who hears the prayers of a praying church. Thank you for praying all night and searching for our son."

"You're most welcome!" the pastor replied. "Praise God for His goodness and mercy." From that day onward, Adek's parents became believing Christians.

As told by George Munson.

CHAPTER 4

A Friend Indeed!

UCKY, LUCKY ME," Wally told himself half aloud. He climbed out of his car at the fish packing plant in Coos Bay, Oregon. He had just completed his freshman college year, and found a summer job three days after school ended. Happily, he bounced up the plant steps to report his arrival. Just inside the door he paused, ran his fingers through his sandy hair, and briskly walked through the first open door. There the steady rhythm of typewriter keys greeted him. He moved toward the busy typist.

"Good morning and what may I do for you?" she asked with a smile.

"I'm Wally. I'm reporting for work." He stood tall and smiled shyly.

"Follow me and I'll introduce you to the foreman," she said as she led the way farther into the plant. The pungent odor of fish nearly choked Wally as they entered the main packing area.

"This is Wally, the new man you were expecting this morning," she told the foreman, and returned to her work.

"Hi, glad to see you, Wally. I need you to help load boxes of ice-packed fish into this van," foreman John said. "As soon as the van is full, I want you to deliver it to Seattle. The secretary will give you the exact address before you leave."

Out in the open air, Wally found the persistent fish smell less stifling. After the foreman helped him load a few boxes, he gave further instructions on how he wanted the van loaded and left Wally on his own. By noon the van was half full. Wally gulped down his sandwich and finished loading. He got the Seattle address and final delivery orders.

Proudly he climbed into the GMC 4-cylinder diesel truck and turned on the ignition. The engine sputtered, roared, and sank into a steady drone. He began his northward trip. He had worked hard loading the fish all day. Weariness engulfed him. He fought to keep awake.

Near midnight, sleep overpowered him. It was the darkest night he had ever seen—no moon or stars in sight. The monotonous motor hum and the unending road's center line hypnotized him. He dozed and forgot to shift to a lower gear on a sharp incline. The motor's lag startled him into reality. Sharply he corrected the front wheels away from the edge of the road and dark abyss. Wally rolled down the window hoping that the cool night air would awaken him. From out of nowhere a Ford station wagon suddenly pulled up beside him.

"Are you all right?" called the friendly logger in plaid shirt and jeans as he stuck his head out of the station wagon window and smiled at Wally. Never before had Wally seen such beautiful white teeth framed by a smile.

"Yes, I'm all right. Just got a bit sleepy," Wally replied. The station wagon sped on ahead of the van. Suddenly just in front of him, the Ford's taillights vanished. Wally searched the road ahead for taillights, but there were none!

"Strange! Whatever happened to the station wagon with those bright taillights?" Wally mused aloud. "How could I lose sight of those taillights on this straight stretch of road? Could it be? Could it really be my guardian angel friend?" he asked, now wide awake with excitement. He'd heard of experiences like that, but they always happened to someone else. Could it have really happened to him?

He delivered the loaded van of fish safely. All summer he loaded and hauled fish, but he never forgot the first night he fought sleep and the smiling stranger in the station wagon—a friend indeed! Wally is a firsthand believer in, "The angel of the Lord encampeth round about them that fear him, and delivereth them" (Psalm 34:7).

As told by Myron Baybarz.
Published by Evangel, *June 3, 1984, and* Purpose, *June 29, 1986.*

CHAPTER 5

Lucky Coincidence?

HE BURST OF DAWN promised another sunny May day. At 5:00 A.M. I slipped to my knees and prayed, "Dear Lord, you know how I dread this lonely trip to Canada today because Highway 17 is torn up for repair. Please go with me. When I stop at Dry Falls, have someone there to guide me around Highway 17 to Mansfield." Peace filled my heart as I arose from my knees and dressed.

The reason for my concern? I recalled my previous trip to Canada to visit Mother in the nursing home. Just north of Dry Falls, I found Highway 17 torn up with rocks and dirt over the entire road. Boulders scraped the bottom of my car. I remember praying, "Lord, please keep me from losing my muffler or causing damage to the bottom of my car."

Meanwhile the woman roadworker with the flag persistently motioned me through the debris. The crew worked to widen and repair the twenty-mile stretch of highway. Certain they'd be on that job all summer, I hoped to avoid that stretch of road this trip.

After my morning prayer, committing my day to my Father above, I knew I would travel in the Best of Hands. On previous trips, He took me safely through the sagebrush and sands of eastern Washington. I knew He'd go with me now.

I studied my map to see if I could find a road leading to Mansfield and bypass Highway 17. The map showed a spiderweb of roads between the Dry Falls rest area and Mansfield.

"Lord, I don't know which of these roads to take without getting lost. Please have someone at Dry Falls who can show me the best way to go," I prayed again.

At Dry Falls Museum, I noticed an unusually large number of excited school children chattering. A blond lady met me with a smile.

Confirming that she was a local resident, I asked, "Can you give me directions to Mansfield so I can miss Highway 17's construction?"

"I'm sorry, I can't give you directions, but our school bus driver can help you, I'm sure. We brought our fifth and sixth graders here for a field trip before the school year ends in a few days," she said and pointed to the bus parked behind some trees. I stepped to her side and saw the big yellow school bus.

"Thank you," I said and walked toward the bus praying, "Thank You, Lord."

A stocky, red-faced man sat in the driver's seat. As I approached him, I asked, "Could you give me directions to Mansfield in order to bypass Highway 17's construction? I'm heading for Canada."

"You bet! You don't want to take Highway 17. It's a mess!" He reached for a piece of paper on the dashboard. "I'll draw you a map to follow. Mind you, it's a gravel road and you won't be travelling fast." He carefully sketched a map for me with precise instructions.

"Thank you so much!" I said and took the "Daily Log-Bus Operations" paper with his hand-drawn map on the blank side. Back in my car, with hands on the steering wheel, I bowed my head, "Thank You, Father, for hearing my prayer and for having the Mansfield school bus driver here at Dry Falls when I needed directions."

To this day, I've kept that map to remind me of my Heavenly Father's care and goodness. I know He directed my trip that day, so I'd meet the Mansfield school group at the precise time I needed special directions. To me it's more than a lucky coincidence. God knew my need before I'd prayed that morning and had it all arranged! His promise in Isaiah 65:24 is sure: "And it shall come to pass that before they call, I will answer; and while they are yet speaking, I will hear."

CHAPTER 6

On Angel Wings

 AWOKE AT 5:00 A.M. and peeked out to find the big July sun rising with scorching promise.

"Are you planning to leave now?" my sleepy husband Marvin asked.

"After I eat and pack the car, I'll be on my way." I pressed a firm kiss on his cheek.

"Drive carefully," he said. "I washed the car and filled the tank on my way home from the ranch last night."

"Thank you! You're always so thoughtful," I whispered with a hug. "I hate to leave. You've been away three weeks for harvest." My voice quavered. "Seems like we've been apart more than we've been together the past four years. But Mother needs me. She's deteriorating fast in that nursing home."

"This, too, shall pass," Marvin said with a sigh.

"Say a prayer for my safe trip. I want to head north before it gets hot."

Hurriedly, I dressed, ate, and packed my ready suitcases into our '69 Buick. Before I backed out of the garage, I prayed, "Dear God, please keep me safe on those 330 miles today. Don't let me have car trouble or an accident. Thank You."

A short way down the road, I heard a *click* which I never heard on previous trips to Canada. I hesitated at the STOP sign—pondering, shall I turn back and tell my husband, or shall I go on my way?

"Mother needs my help," I told myself. "Besides, Marvin always keeps the car in good condition. He surely would have heard that *click* on his way home last evening and told me about it."

"Maybe that constant noise will keep me awake so I won't drive off the road," I positively reasoned as the *click* continued.

My motor purred as I passed the lush hay and potato fields. Overhead sprinklers gushed gallons onto the hot and thirsty vegetation. *Click! Click!* The *click* near the right floor board continued. I sped by golden grain and fragrant mint fields, past sage, and rock-covered terrain. Soon I found a dozen farms where combines like hungry monsters gobbled up ripened grain. I felt secure. If I needed help with my car, farmers are apt mechanics.

Beyond the farms, I cruised through more desert to the louder rhythm of the *click*. I prayed, "Lord, please don't let me have car trouble along this barren country." Next I cruised by mouth-watering apple orchards in northern Washington.

At the Canadian border, dread gripped me. With bated breath, I nosed my car into the last eighty miles of mountainous roads. "Thank You, Lord, for Your protection during the last five hours. Please, go with me the rest of the way," I pleaded. "Lord, You've always been with me on these monthly trips. Please keep my car from a breakdown now."

I shoved my car into low gear. My car labored up the steep grade. We *clicked* over more winding highway, past orchards and lakes. "Thank You, Lord, for the safe trip," I sighed aloud as I finally parked in front of the nursing home.

Wearily, I walked to Mother's bedside. "Glad to see you, Mom." I hugged her. I'm sure her speechless tongue would have told me how glad she was to see me, but many strokes left her mute and paralyzed.

"She always brightens up when you come," her nurse told me as we put her into the wheelchair.

"Let's go outside for some sunshine before supper, Mom," I said and pushed her through the door, along the walkway, passed a rusty, one-horse plough, disk, and hay mower.

"These antique machines remind us of our farming days long ago in northern Alberta, don't they, Mom?"

After I fed Mom supper, read to her, and tucked her in for the night, I drove the three miles of winding mountain road with steep embankments to my brother's home where I stayed.

"Heard a *clicking* in your right back wheel as you drove by to turn around and park," my brother greeted. "Maybe there's a rock under the hubcap." He removed the hubcap—no rock! "Wonder what caused that noise?" He ventured.

"I don't know. It's haunted me all day. I'm going to call Marvin and ask if he heard it on his way home last night."

After the phone call, I told my brother, "Marvin said he had the radio on and didn't hear the *click*. He told me to just 'go easy on the brakes.'"

After ten days of mountain driving to and from the nursing home to care for mother, I motored over the floating bridge, homeward. The 103-degree afternoon heat wilted me. Exhausted, I sped southward down steep grades lined with lakes.

Just past Chief Joseph Dam, I felt dizzy and weak. A quick glance in the rearview mirror revealed my flushed face. I saw a lady in her yard, and parked under her large tree. "May I rest in the shade on your lawn?" I asked her.

"You may. Are you all right?" She asked as I staggered off the car seat and rested my head on top of the door.

"I'm weak and dizzy, but after a cold drink from my thermos and a rest on your lawn, I'll be okay," I reassured her. I spread my blanket on her lawn and lay down to rest. Hot tears sizzled down my burning cheeks.

"Where are You, God?" I prayed. "Do You really exist? I can't take anymore of these trips; caring for mother, only to leave her in the care of strangers after each visit. Why have You forsaken us? Why do You let Mom suffer on and on? She's been a good Christian all her life, always patient, kind, and unselfish. I'm exhausted and cracking under this strain. Besides, my faith is all but gone."

Suddenly ants crawled over my arm and legs. I stopped my complaining to God, jumped up, and vigorously brushed at the ants.

"You deserved a rest, too." I patted my faithful car. "You needed to cool off just like I did." I thanked the kind lady and noisily *clicked* homeward.

Finally home, my husband met me at our driveway. "I'm so thankful you're safely home." His strong arms enveloped me. "We'll take a look at the old Buick soon. Steve promised to help me check it out," he reassured.

A few days later, my husband and son-in-law took the rear right wheel apart. "Come see what we found," Marvin called. "Look at the twisted casings that are supposed to hold all those loose steel bearings in place," he said, pointing to the roller bearings inside the wheel's center.

"How you made it to Canada and all the way back, I'll never understand!" Marvin exclaimed, and both men shook their heads in disbelief.

"Why?" I naively asked. "What could have happened?"

"The wheel should have come off and you could have rolled the car. How you ever made it, I'll never know!" he said.

"I know how I made it," I said. "On angel wings. I prayed constantly."

Once I entered the house, I prayed again, "Thank You, Lord, for Your protection and love. I needed a faith booster like that. Now I know You *do* exist and care."

CHAPTER 7

An Angel's Touch

'M ON MY WAY HOME, Carolyn, so I won't call you tomorrow night," my husband, Fred, told me on the phone.

"Okay, I'll look for you to come home soon," I told him. He faithfully called whenever he traveled extensively on business trips. To my surprise, the next evening he called anyhow.

"I'm very tired after a long drive today and not feeling the best, so I thought I should tell you. I'm okay though, and on my way home. Hopefully, I'll be home tomorrow," he said.

"All right. Get a good night's rest and have a safe trip," I told him. "I'll be looking for you. Miss you a lot, Fred."

My hard-working, forty-six-year-old husband didn't realize he'd had a small heart attack during his trip home.

When he arrived home, I told him, "My folks invited us over for supper this evening. Do you feel like going? You look exhausted."

"I'll rest a bit. Then we can go," he said. "I can't miss out on your mother's delicious cooking. You know how I like her good food. A drive to the country will be relaxing."

After supper we visited with guests in the living room when Fred arose and left the room. I thought he'd gone to the bathroom. When he didn't return after a long time, concern gripped me. I hurried to investigate.

"I saw him go into the bedroom," one of the guests called after me. There I found Fred lying on the bed—face ashen, pulse weak, and complaining of chest pain.

"Dad, come help me walk Fred to the car," I called. "He's terribly sick."

"I'll call the ambulance to meet you at home," Dad said as he helped Fred into the car. The ambulance—only a vehicle for transportation without life-support equipment in those days—met us at our driveway and rushed Fred to the hospital.

Every evening, I'd go to the hospital to give Fred a back rub and do whatever was necessary to make him comfortable for the night. Worried he'd have a fatal heart attack, I'd come home each evening, get down on my knees to cry and pray and pray and cry. I'd cry myself to sleep every night from fear of losing Fred.

"Dear God, please save Fred and help him recover. You know how much I need him. I can't live without him." Exhausted, I prayed one evening as I knelt weeping beside my bed. Then I felt a warm hand on my shoulder.

"Why are you crying?" an audible voice asked. "He's going to be all right." I quickly arose from my knees and found no one in the room. I crawled into bed and slept soundly all night.

After I awoke the next morning, I asked myself, "How come I slept so well last night and feel rested for a change?" Then I remembered a hand touched my shoulder the evening before and the audible voice reassuring me that Fred would be all right. Every night after that I slept peacefully, believing Fred would fully recover.

Throughout the remainder of his eighty years, he worked hard and enjoyed living. I'll never forget the hand on my shoulder and that audible, reassuring voice during that trying time in my life.

As told by Carolyn Baybarz.

CHAPTER 8

Good-Looking Stranger

CAN HARDLY WAIT for a glass of ice water," my husband Fred said, wiping perspiration from his face. "Besides, I'm starved." With the summer sun ablaze and humidity high, we entered the restaurant after a tiresome drive from California to Grand Rapids, Michigan.

"I'm thirsty and hungry too," I said. "Doesn't the aroma of the potato chips make your mouth water, Fred?"

After a delicious meal in the cool, restful atmosphere, we returned to the parking lot and found our left rear tire completely flat.

"Oh no!" I gasped, because our trunk was full of suitcases. We both were tired and I worried, because Fred had suffered a heart attack several months before and wasn't feeling well. To unload the trunk, get the spare tire from under the suitcases, and change the tire would cause him more stress.

As Fred opened the trunk and we began unloading, a nice-looking, well-dressed man approached us.

"Are you having problems?" he asked.

"We have a flat tire," Fred muttered.

"Let me help you," he said, removing his gray business-suit jacket. Folding it carefully, he placed it on the hood of our car.

Saying nothing more, he removed the remaining suitcases and stacked them neatly. He pulled out the spare tire, pumped it up, removed the flat, and tightened the spare in place. After reloading all the suitcases, he picked up his jacket and slipped it on. We closed the trunk and turned to thank him. He was gone!

"Where did he go?" I asked.

"I don't know!" Fred looked around puzzled. "There aren't any cars parked near us and we're a long way from buildings."

"How could he have disappeared so quickly?"

"It's a mystery!" Fred scanned the empty parking lot again. "I didn't hear a motor start anywhere. Did you?"

"No! I didn't. Do you suppose that good-looking stranger was an angel sent to help us since you weren't feeling well?"

"You're right," Fred said. "He must have been an angel."

With high spirits, thankful hearts, and renewed faith in our Heavenly Father's loving care, we drove to our motel for a restful night. All evening we talked about the kindness of that good-looking stranger.

As told by Carolyn Baybarz.

CHAPTER 9

Divine Guidance

 NEED DRAPES," I told my new friend, a faculty member, one morning.

"I'll take you shopping," she said, staring at our bare living room windows. "I plan to go to Portland today anyway. I'm sure you'll find the drapes you need at the shopping center."

"Thank you!" I responded. We'd recently moved to Columbia Academy, near Vancouver, Washington, from Wisconsin. I was unfamiliar with the area or the town of Portland and welcomed her kind offer.

"I want you to drive my car," I told her.

"I'd rather drive my car."

"No, I insist you drive my car. If anything happens, I'd rather have it happen to my car than yours, because it's older."

"All right, we'll take your car, if you insist," she said.

Two academy girls went shopping with us and rode in the back seat. About ten miles from the shopping center, the driver of a flat-nosed diesel truck barreled past us. He didn't realize his trailer had unhitched and kept on driving, while the trailer loaded with heavy wooden cement forms crossed the center line and headed toward our car.

"Take the ditch and the field!" I screamed. Our driver froze. With knuckles white and fingers tightly wrapped around the steering wheel, she headed toward the unguided trailer.

In spite of her firm grip on the wheel, I grabbed it and forced the car toward the ditch, but not in time. Crash! The trailer hit the back of our car and threw the front end against its load. Without seat belts fastened, the girls bounced forward. One girl lacerated her scalp from front to back on the door clothes hook. Blood gushed everywhere.

"Dear Lord," I prayed, "What shall I do?"

Before these words were out of my mouth, a strong voice urged, "Apply pressure to her neck and stop the bleeding!" Without first-aid training, I followed the instruction and immediately applied pressure to both sides of her neck. Unhurt, the rest of us moved the injured girl from the car, placing her on the ground in the nearby field.

"Go to that house at the end of the field," I told the other girl and driver. "Get some ice and clean rags." Although still shaking, they hurried across the field while I continued applying pressure. Soon the girl returned with ice and clean towels, which we applied to the injury. Our driver remained at the house to call an ambulance and her husband. In a short time, the ambulance arrived and whisked the injured girl to the hospital.

"You ladies are lucky you weren't hit head-on," the policeman told us, pointing to the trailer. "You could have slid under this loaded trailer and all been killed."

Meanwhile at the hospital, the emergency room doctor put in the final stitches, and told our injured friend, "That woman did the right thing to stop your bleeding. I'll check your X rays and make sure there are no hidden injuries." He left the room and later returned.

"Your X rays look fine, young woman," he squeezed her hand. "You're a lucky girl that your injuries weren't serious."

Later, with a tight hug, the student thanked me for saving her life.

"I'm glad we took my car," I told our driver. "I'm also glad that I asked God to guide me through the day's activities according to His will this morning before I started my day. I'm sure the Holy Spirit or an angel gave me guidance during that emergency."

"I'm sure He did, and I'm thankful that no one was seriously injured," our driver agreed.

As told by Rose McChesney.

CHAPTER 10

Two Unusual Awakenings

THUNDERING ROAR from the potbellied stove's chimney startled me. I ran outside to find flames, like Fourth of July fireworks, shooting from our brick chimney. I raced to the barn shouting, "The chimney's on fire! Come quickly!" My husband and the dairy helpers ran toward the house. There wasn't anything they could do but watch, with hoses ready, in case the roof caught fire. After the soot quit burning, the men returned to work.

We had just moved to Oregon. With our boxes and furniture heaped in the dining room, adjacent to the potbellied stove, I shampooed the living room rug. When finished, I lit the stove to hasten the rug-drying process. That's when the chimney caught fire.

That evening I unpacked, organized, and put dishes into clean cupboards. Since my husband arose at 1:30 A.M. to care for dairy cattle, he retired early. But before he crawled into bed, he opened the attic door opposite our bedroom and checked the chimney. Everything appeared all right since the chimney fire.

Exhausted, I dropped into bed at 11:30 P.M. and fell fast asleep. Suddenly, I felt myself being raised into a sitting position. I blinked, peered into the darkness and heard crackling. I stared at the ceiling—I could see it smoldering! With our door closed and window open, I didn't smell smoke.

"Wake up! Wake up!" I screamed and violently shook my husband. "The house is on fire!"

"Grab the kids!" he shouted, turned on the light, and jumped out of bed. I jerked the door open. Blue smoke filled the hallway. Dashing across the hall to our daughter's room, I found her, blankets pulled over her head, and yanked her out of bed.

"Wake up!" I yelled, and shoved her toward her dad. Coughing, I tore down the hall and jerked our sleepy son from his bed. "The house is on fire!" I shouted in his ear. We hustled the children downstairs, out of the house, and into the car. Quickly, I drove them to nearby neighbors while my husband called the fire department.

Returning, I found firemen dousing ferocious flames. I thought, *Oh, dear! If they pour water on that fire, it's going to soak our unpacked things in the dining room right below the fire.* What did I do? I charged into the house. With super strength, I pulled my heavy, old-fashioned piano from the dining area into the living room.

With the fire extinguished, firemen concluded that old, dry wood next to the hot bricks smoldered and ignited. The charred two-by-fours around the chimney had to be replaced and the sooty house cleaned. Our family gratefully thanked God for miraculously awakening me in time to save our family.

Another night, while still living in Wisconsin, I felt myself being lifted to a sitting position from a sound sleep. Sitting, I faced the window and saw light in the barn.

"Honey, you overslept," I said, shaking my husband, the dairy manager for the Academy. "The other fellows are down at the barn. It's all lit up!"

He raised to his elbow and stared at the clock. "It's too early! It's not even midnight." He jumped out of bed, yanked on his overalls, grabbed a flashlight and raced downstairs to awaken the farm manager, who lived next door.

"Oh, dear!" I worried. "What if someone hits them over the head." My heart raced. My eyes pierced the darkness. I strained to see them walk toward the barn, but couldn't. When I went to the bathroom and turned on the light, the lights went out in the barn.

At the back of the barn's double doors, a cattle truck droned and then roared toward the adjacent highway. Two pickups sped after the truck and turned in opposite directions. When I turned on the bathroom light, I must have spooked the cattle thieves.

Due to my unusual awakening, we didn't lose our cattle that night. Later we learned that a neighbor, about a half-mile away, lost cattle to rustlers a few nights previous.

As told by Rose McChesney.

CHAPTER 11

The Vanishing Snowplow

Y HEART BEAT IN MY CHEST like a pounding hammer. Puffing, I gasped the cold morning air. "Maybe it wasn't a smart idea to shovel thirteen inches of heavy, new snow from my driveway." I told myself.

Exhausted, I leaned on my shovel to rest. "How can I muster the strength necessary to shovel the snow heaped at my driveway entrance by the snowplow?" I asked myself. With a heart problem, I knew better than to push myself and keep shoveling.

I had promised my neighbor, Mary, we would deliver the Bible lessons this morning to eleven addresses we'd obtained at prayer meeting. In order to drive my car onto the roadway, I needed to remove the two-foot mountain of snow blocking my driveway. With my husband in the nursing home, the only helping hand available was the one at the end of my sleeve.

"Thank You, Lord, for strength to shovel my driveway." I prayed. "Please give me strength to clear the entrance so I can get my car onto the plowed road."

While I rested on my shovel, my pounding heart slowed, and the roar of a motor caught my attention. Looking down the street, I saw a tractor with a scoop turn around and lumber toward me. Smiling, the middle-aged driver dropped his scoop and lifted all the snow from my driveway entrance. He backed away, waved, and drove toward our housing-complex exit. But once there, he didn't turn right or left onto the main highway. I stared and listened—no motor, no tractor, no scoop loaded with snow! How could he have disappeared while I watched?

"Thank You, Lord," I prayed, "for sending help when I needed it so desperately."

After I shoveled my sidewalk, I walked around the corner to see if Mary was ready to help me find the addresses of the people who requested Bible lessons.

When I arrived at Mary's house, I discovered she didn't have her snow shoveled. As I stood at the curb pondering how I could best climb the bank bordering her yard without falling, a pickup raced around the corner.

"You have no business going that fast on these icy roads," I scolded the driver as I watched the pickup disappear around the corner. I looked in the opposite direction and saw a man in a brown jacket standing about three feet from me.

"I see you need some help," he said. "Let me help you." With his high-topped shoe, he swung his foot from side to side, brushing the snow into a path up the bank.

"Now give me your hand and I'll help you up the path." Ordinarily, I wouldn't give my hand to a strange man, but I took his hand. He pulled me up the slippery bank. At the top, I gratefully squeezed his hand, released it, and opened my mouth to thank him. He was gone! I looked all around. He was nowhere in sight!

Overwhelmed and dumbfounded, I stood fixed to the path that he had just made for me. Then I raced to Mary's door and knocked. I told her of both the vanishing snowplow and the disappearing stranger.

"See! Here's the path he made for me," I pointed. "Could it be that I held and squeezed my guardian angel's hand, Mary?"

"It could be!" Amazed, Mary stood staring at the fresh path in the snow.

"Get your map, Mary. Maybe the reason I received all that providential help this morning is because we need to deliver those Bible lessons *today*!"

As told by Rose McChesney.

Bible Studies by an Angel

N 1994, A CHURCH MISSIONS ORGANIZATION in the Ethiopian city of Addis Ababa received an urgent call for a pastor to be sent to another city. Surprise gripped the men at the Union office, for they knew of no church members or missionaries in that particular city. They immediately sent a pastor to a specific address in that town.

When the pastor arrived at the given address, he met a tall, wealthy sheik.

"I'm so glad you've come!" Smiling, the sheik extended his hand. "Will you baptize me and many of my people?" he asked.

"Sir, you don't understand!" the bewildered pastor answered. "We don't baptize anyone until we have carefully studied all our Bible doctrines with them."

"Pastor, I know all the church doctrines. You see, for many months an angel came to study the Bible with me. He taught me this beautiful Bible message. I have taught these truths to my people, and now we are all ready for baptism."

"Could you call your people together for a meeting today?" the pastor asked the sheik.

"Oh, yes," he said. Soon his home overflowed with people requesting baptism. After much discussion with the group, the pastor found their knowledge of Bible doctrines sound and true. Before he returned to the Union office that day, the pastor baptized as many people as he could.

Excited, the pastor related this story to his co-workers at the Union office. He asked them, "Could it be that angels are doing the work entrusted to us humans? Are we truly about our Father's business as we should be? The end is nearer than any of us realize. Jesus is coming sooner than most of us think."

As told by Martha Toews.

C H A P T E R   1 3

The Talking Buffalo

OST PEOPLE IN ASIA are rice farmers. Each family owns a patch of ground in which they plant rice. Since the production of rice needs a lot of moisture, they build mud walls around each field to retain the water in that paddy. Some farmers own a water buffalo. This animal plows fields, pulls carts, and provides milk for the family. They usually keep these buffalo tethered when they are not working.

On one of the islands, a farmer had just planted his rice crop when he looked up and saw a large buffalo lumber toward his field. That animal actually walked into his rice patch and broke his mud wall.

"Who does that animal belong to?" he asked himself. "I haven't seen him before." Waving his arms, he yelled, "Shoo! Shoo! Get out of my field, you big beast!" After the animal ambled away, the farmer returned to his work.

A short time later, he looked and saw that buffalo walking toward him again. "Here comes that beast!" he muttered and grabbed a stick to chase the buffalo from his field for the second time. Instead of promptly leaving as he did before, the buffalo turned, faced the farmer, opened his big mouth and said, "The Lord is coming soon! The Lord is coming soon!" After he'd said that, he turned and walked peacefully away. He was never seen again.

"How strange!" The farmer said aloud. He couldn't believe what he'd just seen and heard. He fixed the broken wall and hurried home to tell his wife about the speaking buffalo's message.

"Let's not tell anyone about this experience," the farmer told his wife. "If we tell people, they'll think we're crazy!"

"Okay," she agreed, but they could not forget this unusual experience.

Meanwhile, in their village, religious meetings were in progress, conducted by young theology students from the college. Up to this time, the farmer and his wife were uninterested in attending.

One day the farmer said to his wife, "Let's go and hear what the young preachers are saying. It won't hurt to go just one time." His wife agreed, and they decided to attend only once.

To their surprise, the young preacher spoke that evening about Jesus' soon coming. After the meeting, this farmer could no longer refrain from telling his experience with the talking water buffalo, who gave him the same message as the young evangelist did. He told the evangelist and shared his story with the villagers. His unusual experience had a great impact on all of them. He and his wife continued to attend all of the remaining meetings and believed the evangelist's message was from God's word.

As a result, today there is a church in that village. They all praise God for the "unusual" talking buffalo and for the evangelistic meetings conducted by the college theology students.

As told by Martha Toews.

CHAPTER 14

God's Affirmative

EAR GOD, I'M AFRAID TO SLEEP. I may never wake up. Why did I get sick? Please make morning come soon. Please make me well," I gasped from my hospital bed while moist oxygen hissed through the mask over my nose.

The nurse placed a cold cloth on my hot forehead, a heating pad on my chest, and the On-Off control in my hand. "When it gets too hot, turn it off," she said. "I don't want you to burn."

Although the heat eased my chest pain, it soon became too hot. Painfully my swollen thumb struggled to push the switch off. Every joint ached. I could not turn it by myself. Alone and weary, I stared into the darkness and recalled the events of the past few months—including high school graduation. I had planned to attend college that fall, but....

"The crops look poor. There won't be any money for college," I remembered Dad telling me. I prayed for a job and got a nurse aide position at this hospital. Every challenging minute that I cared for the sick cinched my decision to become a nurse. I planned to work a year and save toward college, and now this.

At last, dawn crept through my window and ended the longest night I ever

38

knew. Exhausted, I tried to catch the next breath, and the next and the next. . . .

"Good morning. How are you?" Dr. Ray asked as he came to my bedside.

"Every joint in my body aches," I said wearily. "I can't move. What's the matter with me, Doctor?"

"Sorry, I don't know. A few more laboratory tests should give me a diagnosis." With that comment he disappeared.

"Dear God, I hurt so. Please don't let me die. I'm not through living yet. I want to become a nurse someday." My parched lips quivered.

"Lynn," a gentle hand touched my arm. Ruth, the nurse, spoke, "Your doctor, Pastor Smith, and I have come to have special prayer for you." I opened my eyes momentarily to see them kneeling at my bedside. Pastor Smith prayed briefly and fervently for my recovery.

"Thank you," I said with effort as they arose and left. How wonderful to have a Christian doctor and nurses to care for me, I thought.

Later Dr. Ray returned with two other physicians. After a thorough exam and discussion, he told me, "You have acute rheumatic fever complicated by pleurisy. We are doing all we can to help you. We thought your parents should know and called them. Your father is on his way to see you."

"Can you please give me something for pain?" I asked. "My joints ache unbearably." After an injection, I lay senseless the rest of the day. At midnight, shivering and drenched in perspiration, I struggled to find the call bell.

"I'm breathing easier and my joints don't hurt as much," I told the two nurses who quickly removed the oxygen and changed my bed and gown.

"Let's check your temperature. Your hips and knees look less swollen," Nurse Marie said. She placed the thermometer under my tongue. A few minutes later she removed it and checked it.

"Hurray! It's down—101 is better than 105 degrees." After that I slept peacefully until my breakfast tray arrived.

"I don't know when applesauce and toast tasted so good," I told Nurse Ruth, when she picked up my tray.

"I'm glad you're feeling better this morning. Your father is here to see you," she said as Dad stepped into the room.

"My child! How are you?" Dad hugged me. Tears of joy washed both our faces. "After the phone call, I waited at the airport, hoping for a cancelled seat, but there was none. When I boarded the slow, midnight bus, I asked God to spare your life. I knew He would. You're better, aren't you?"

"Yes, Daddy, I'm better, and so glad to see you. At midnight my temperature suddenly dropped and my joints weren't as painful. Your prayer was answered! How's Mom?"

"She wasn't feeling the best. That's why she didn't come."

From that day onward, I slowly grew stronger. Five days later, I greeted my doctor, "Daddy's going home today. May I go with him?"

"You've made a remarkable recovery, but you are not well enough to travel that far. Now that you're stronger, I will tell you more about your condition. You illness left your heart damaged. That means bed rest for several months. I've already explained this to your father."

"Bed rest? Several months? I won't be able to go back to work?" I sat straight up, but fell back into my pillow.

"Your complete recovery depends on how well you rest to give your heart a chance to heal," my doctor told me and left the room. I buried my face in the pillow and cried.

"Now, Lynn," Father said, stroking my tousled brown hair. "God heard our prayers and spared your life. I believe you will fully recover. God never leaves a job half done. Rest and do as the doctor says. He'll let you come home when you're stronger." He paused, studied the floor, and looked at me. "I hate to say goodbye, but I have to catch the bus home."

Three weeks later, my doctor told me, "You may go home today, but keep off your feet and rest. Be sure to see your own doctor in a few weeks. The nurse will give you a supply of medicine to take with you."

At home, under a local doctor's care, the "several months" grew into two years. Depression overtook me. Daily, I began reading my Bible and claimed the promise, "Wait on the Lord: be of good courage, and He shall strengthen thine heart" (Psalm 27:14).

"Dear God," I prayed one day. "I believe You can heal me. I claim this promise as my very own." Finally the depression left and I grew stronger.

A few weeks later, I saw my doctor who had ordered blood tests and chest X rays. He told me, "Your blood tests are all normal and the X rays show a normal-sized heart. A slight murmur remains, but you can live a normal life."

"Really, Doctor? I feel like a bird out of a cage. I'm so happy!" Winged feet carried me from the doctor's office. "Dear God, how can I thank You enough for hearing my prayers!" I whispered.

Today a college graduate and a registered nurse, I continue to thank God for His positive answer to many prayers during that time in my life.

CHAPTER 15

When God Intervenes

AD, DO YOU KNOW what I plan to do after graduation?" Sharon asked, her blue eyes sparkling.

"No, what?" Dad put down his magazine and faced her.

"Linda and I are going to Chicago to take a nine-month travel agent course," she said. Dad raised his eyebrows.

"Dad, just think! After nine months, I can work in an airport selling tickets. That would be a fun job!"

"It's natural for you to sprout wings, Sharon, and I can see why a short course and job possibility appeal to you. But Linda isn't a Christian. Her values and habits are vastly different from ours. Besides, going to that big city wouldn't be the safest adventure."

"Don't talk to me about values anymore, Dad. My mind is made up and I've already sent my application and deposit. Class begins soon after graduation."

Mother stopped flipping pancakes. She and Dad exchanged silent glances. They knew if they further opposed, Sharon would be even more determined to pursue her plans.

"Maybe you should give that decision more careful thought," Mother added and turned another pancake. After that, Sharon's parents daily asked

God to intervene in her decision according to His will.

Meanwhile, Sharon returned to academy and finished her senior year. Two weeks before graduation, her class took a trip to Vancouver Island. A senior class party at Kathy's house climaxed the evening of their return. Kathy's folks had given her an early graduation gift—a gold convertible coupe!

"Since it's so nice out, let's try my new car," Kathy suggested as her classmates admired it.

"It's neat!" Joe said and kicked a tire.

"It's so beautiful, Kathy," Sharon slid her hand across the shiny door and smiled.

"Here, give it a run," Kathy tossed the keys to Sharon. Others had already tried the coupe and all talked at once about its beauty and performance.

"Thanks, Kathy," Sharon's eyes sparkled as she hopped behind the wheel.

"If you don't mind, I'll ride with you, Sharon," Joe said and slid onto the seat beside her.

"Okay, Joe," Sharon said and turned the key. The engine roared and then purred. They sped through their small academy town. *Clank, Clank!* Over the wooden bridge, and along a familiar country road. Her foot pushed the gas pedal to fifty, fifty-five, then sixty miles per hour. A full moon silhouetted fence posts guarding pastures.

"Boy, you sure drive good for a girl," Joe teased, as trees whizzed past.

"Thanks!" Sharon laughed. "The class trip and this party have been such fun. I feel so carefree and at home with my classmates. They're so different."

"Don't you think it's because our values are the same?" Joe asked. The road grew unfamiliar as they talked. A sharp, unexpected turn leaped at them. Sharon turned the wheel. Speed resisted her efforts, and she overcorrected.

"Look out!" Joe shouted. Crash! A fence post snapped. The car narrowly missed a tree. A bush caught the coupe and held it fast. Sharon lay motionless, her head in Joe's lap. Joe sat stunned. Finally she sat up.

"Now I've ruined Kathy's new car! My head hurts," she moaned. She brushed her hand across her eyes. The moonlight reflected red on her fingers.

"Are you hurt, Joe?

"I'm okay. At least we're alive. I think the blood on my pants is from your head. Let's get out of here," Joe said, struggling to open the door against resisting bushes.

Sharon's teeth chattered, "Give me a few minutes to quit shaking."

"I see lights at a nearby farm. Let's get help," Joe said and pulled quivering Sharon from the wreckage.

"My legs are okay, Joe, but what does my face look like?" Sharon gripped Joe's arm.

"You've got quite a lot of blood on your face. Let's get to that farmhouse." Sharon leaned on his arm as they inched their way through the bushes, climbed the embankment, and staggered onto the road.

"Soon we'll be at the farm house." Joe opened the gate.

"I'm scared. Let's not stop here. Let's walk back to Kathy's house. I don't want to be seen like this. I think we can make it back if you help me, Joe." Sharon stood, unmoving. Reluctantly, Joe closed the gate. Sharon's steps slowed as Joe supported her. For three miles they snail-paced. They arrived at Kathy's home very late.

"What happened?" their friends asked as they entered.

"I'm so sorry I wrecked your car, Kathy," Sharon said.

"We ran off the road," Joe told them, releasing Sharon into friendly hands. They hustled her into the bathroom. When Sharon passed the mirror and saw her face, she fainted. Once revived, classmates cleaned her face, but stopped at her gashed hairline.

"You'd best go to the emergency room," Kathy told Sharon.

"Oh, I'll be all right now," Sharon said.

"Come on. We have a car ready to take you," Joe insisted.

Later, the emergency room doctor diagnosed a concussion and a skull fracture. "Admit her for observation tonight," he told the nurse.

"Oh no," Sharon groaned, but they ignored her resistance. The hospital bustle frightened her. She spent the night in a crowded hallway. Her head throbbed.

"What will Kathy think? I wrecked her car! How did I get into this mess? Why did I ever drive that car?" she repeatedly asked herself. "Why did this happen?"

The next morning the doctor told her, "I've decided to keep you in the hospital for a few days. You need complete bed rest."

Later that afternoon her parents visited. "What happened?" Dad asked.

"We took turns driving Kathy's new car! While I drove, we went off the road." Her fingers fidgeted with the blanket. "I'm to stay here about—what was I going to say? I forgot...."

"Don't try to talk. You can tell us about it later," Mother squeezed her hand. "We love you and are glad you weren't hurt any worse or killed."

After three days in the hospital, Sharon returned to classes. With rest between studies, she managed to complete her school year and finals.

"You may march for graduation, but you need a quiet summer. That means rest, no strenuous activity, job or classes," the doctor told Sharon during a follow-up visit.

"But I've already enrolled in a summer course," she persisted.

"No job or classes, understand?" her doctor said and left the room.

On the evening of graduation Sharon stood among classmates—ready to march. Their Christian friendship and influence meant much to her. She felt happy and sad all at once. Happy to have recovered so she could march with them, and sad because within hours their ways would lead many directions.

Sharon followed her doctor's advice and rested all summer. Later, she said, "I knew God shook me up in that car accident to give me time to think before making a major decision in my life. Every time I see the scar on my forehead, I think of how God intervened in answer to my parents' prayers and I'm glad He did."

Today, a Christian, Sharon is a school secretary and has many opportunities to counsel young people in making decisions.

As told by Sharon Hibbs.

CHAPTER 16

Angel in the Woods

ONNIE, ANN'S TEENAGED SISTER, placed her arm across Mother's shoulders. "Thanks for the yummy breakfast, Mom! You make the best pancakes!"

Mother's caring eyes met Bonnie's. "You're welcome!" Bonnie gathered dirty dishes from the table and carried them to the sink. "I really appreciate your help with the dishes, and your care of your brother, and three little sisters."

"May we go out to play, Mom?" Randy interrupted.

"Yes, Mommy, may we?" Seven-year-old Ann jumped up and down.

Mother hesitated. "Yes, you may, but please stay in the yard." She loved and cared for her five children and didn't want them far from home in a new neighborhood. With their father in Korea, they were her entire responsibility. Army life meant frequent moves for their family and many living adjustments.

Through the window, Mother watched Randy and Ann play tag in the front yard while she dressed Mary, age four, and Jinny, two years. Soon other daily chores captured her attention.

"Let's go play in the woods," Randy pointed down the street and started across the road.

Ann paused at the road's edge, looked both ways and shouted, "Mother said to stay in the yard."

"Mother will never know we went," Randy beckoned as he walked backwards. "Come on, Ann, let's go!"

"But mother said. . . ."

"You're just a chicken," Randy interrupted her, and turned toward the woods. "I'll go without you then!"

For a few moments, Ann stood watching him walk down the street. "I can't let him go alone," she told herself. "Wait for me, Randy!" she shouted and bolted after him. "I'm coming with you."

Against the blue sky, birds warbled and winged through budding green branches. In the woods, Ann knelt and buried her nose in fragrant pink flowers. "Let's pick some for Mother, Randy."

"No, silly!"

"Then Mother will know we disobeyed, right?"

"Right! Come on, Ann, quit smelling the flowers. Let's play hide-and-seek. Count to a hundred, and then come and find me."

Slowly Ann counted aloud, "Sixty-five, sixty-six, sixty-seven . . ."

Suddenly she heard Randy screaming, "Help! Help! Help! Ann, Help!" Her feet flew in the direction of his voice. Breathless, she tore through the woods. In a clearing, her jaw dropped. She found Randy ankle-deep in mud, which proved to be quicksand.

"Help me, Ann!" Randy shouted. "Don't just stand there!" The more he twisted and turned, the deeper he sank.

"I'd best not come near you, or I'll get stuck too," she yelled. She knew it was up to her to save him from sinking completely. "I'll run fast and get help."

"Hurry, then!"

Looking down, Ann raced along the wooded path. "Who will I find to help us?" she asked herself. Suddenly she saw two big shoes, then blue jeans in front of her. She looked up to find a strong, handsome young man towering above her. *Where did he come from?* she wondered. His neat attire and friendly face erased her fears.

"Hey, Mister, would you please hurry and help my big brother get out of the mud?"

"Why surely," he said. "Take me to him." Ann turned and both ran back to where Randy struggled.

Gasping, Ann pointed, "There's my brother. Please help him, Mister!"

"Help! Help!" Arms flailing, Randy had sunk to chest deep.

The young man snatched a long stick and reached it toward Randy. "Grab it and hold on tight," he said.

Randy snatched the stick. Effortlessly the stranger quickly pulled him from the quicksand. Frightened and stressed, Randy shook like a leaf in the wind.

"You're a real mess!" Ann told her brother as the three of them stood surveying the situation. "Now Mother will know we disobeyed her, right?"

"I don't care!" Randy cried. "I just want to go home." Like a frightened rabbit, he darted down the path toward home.

Ann's eyes, as big as dinner plates, followed her muddy brother's form as it disappeared among the trees. She turned to thank the kind, young man for saving her brother. He was nowhere in sight. *I wonder where he went*, she asked herself and looked everywhere but couldn't find him. Frightened, she also raced home. Ann doesn't remember being punished, but when she arrived in the front yard, she found Mother hosing Randy with cold water.

To this day, forty years later, Ann believes the kind, young man who saved her brother was Randy's guardian angel sent to save him from suffocation in the quicksand.

"We thank our loving heavenly Father for guardian angels who help us in unexpected ways even when we disobey," Ann said in telling this story. "Are they not all ministering spirits, sent forth to minister for them who shall be heirs of salvation" (Hebrews 1:14).

As told by Ann Schwalbach.

CHAPTER 17

Visitor at Dawn

EERING OVER MY HUSBAND'S SHOULDER, I silently read the surgical consent he studied. "Are you going to sign that form?" I asked. "It sounds like risky business to me." I pointed. "Look at those words: 'possible vision loss, bleeding, and perhaps even death'!"

Walking around to face my husband, I searched his gaze. "Honey, do you really want to go through with this surgery?"

He sighed and flicked the paper he held. "I don't have much choice, do I? I can't go on living the way I have the past few months. This continuous hammering in my ear will drive me crazy." Two days later, I followed my husband's gurney to the big, double doors of surgery.

"This is as far as you may go," the nurses told me. With finality the doors shut behind nurses, gurney, and my precious husband. Through the narrow window on the door, I watched the procession recede down the hallway and out of sight.

Numb and alone, I stood there. "Dear Lord, You know the risks of this endoscopic sinus surgery better than I do. Please give the surgeon steady hands so that my husband will come through it all right. I commit him into

Your care. I can't live without him, You know." My prayers continued as I paced the cold hospital hallways.

After three hours, my husband finally returned to his hospital room. With both nasal passages packed, his breathing seemed laborious. "Thank God, you made it through surgery, honey!" I bent to kiss his forehead.

"I'm so thirsty!" he whispered.

"I'll get you a glass of water right away." Eagerly his parched lips sipped fresh water. For several hours I watched nurses dart in and out of adjoining rooms caring for the sick while I gave my special patient sips of water and changed ice packs on his nose.

At 6:00 P.M. they discharged us. Once at home, the sips of water and changing ice packs continued throughout the night. We scarcely slept that first night.

Much of the time we take God's life-sustaining love for granted—like rhythmic heartbeat after heartbeat and successive respirations. Once we've lost the effectiveness of these involuntary body functions, stress ensues. That's what happened to my husband. Postoperative trauma, edema and surgical packing made breathing difficult and exhausting for him. Discouragement overtook him.

At dawn, a few days later, I awoke with a start. Fear gripped me. I hesitated to open my eyes. I sensed someone in our bedroom. Listening, I heard only my husband's breathing. *No one could have come into our house with the doors and windows secured*, I told myself.

Slowly, I opened my eyes and saw all our bedroom furniture. I looked at the ceiling light and just below it I saw the tall, slim, white-robed intruder. Standing at my side of the bed, he bent over, looking down on my husband as though checking his respirations. I saw his feathered wing on the side away from me folded against his body. The wing next to me hung lowered and relaxed. His sandy, chin-length hair, curled slightly at the ends, hid his face from my breathless view. Had he stood upright, his head would have touched our ceiling. Suddenly this caring, silent visitor melted into the growing dawn.

The warmth of heavenly peace enveloped me as I lay there. "Thank You, Father in heaven, for Your reassuring visitor this morning. Now I know You've been and will be with us during this difficult time. Thank You for my dear husband's recovery thus far."

Impatiently, I waited for my husband to awaken. I eagerly wished to tell him what I had just seen! He stirred. He reached for his glass of water. I touched his shoulder. "Honey, your guardian angel really loves you," I began. "He just stood on my side of the bed, bent and looked at you as if he were checking your breathing. I saw your angel, honey! He's watching over you!" Tears filled my discouraged husband's eyes. He had endured much through the trial of surgery. Revitalized with courage, we faced the new day.

The next day, we faced a slow hemorrhage, but the doctor stopped the bleeding. Somehow that didn't frighten us, because we knew that our special visitor at dawn the day before stood there beside us. We're promised, "Heavenly angels are at the service of the humble, believing people of God" (*The Acts of the Apostles*, page 154). Furthermore, "Angels of light and power are ever near to protect, to comfort, to heal, to instruct, to inspire" (*Gospel Workers*, page 515).

We can scarcely wait to meet this tall, white-robed visitor on the streets of heaven and personally thank him for coming to boost our sagging, weary spirits during this trying time in our lives.

CHAPTER 18

Unusual Passengers

EOPLE WHO LIVE IN SMALL TOWNS shouldn't drive in large, unfamiliar cities. But I had to attend a seminar in a large coastal city. I'd asked the lady at my travel agency to book a room for me near the seminar building. I told her the seminar was scheduled in the University District, but didn't tell her *which* university. When I arrived, I found I had to drive from my motel across the entire city to locate the university for the seminar.

With good directions, I found the university just fine. But the parking lot supervisor told me I had to go elsewhere to park. "Turn right, here," he pointed. "At the next stop sign, turn right at 12th Avenue. Turn left and then right again to find Broadway." By the time he'd finished giving directions, he'd lost me.

"Would you please repeat the directions?" I asked. "You said I should go back to 12th Avenue. But how do I get back to Twelfth? I can't back up because of the cars behind me now."

"Just go through the parking lot," he motioned.

"That sounds easy," I told him and drove ahead. But I got lost in the parking lot because "one-way" and "dead end" signs allowed me to turn only certain directions. By the time I finally found Twelfth Avenue, I felt totally confused and forgot the original directions given me.

"Let's see," I told myself, "I think he said, 'go down Twelfth and turn right on Broadway and look for the Broadway Parking Garage.' I should be able to find it without a problem."

After driving nearly two miles, I found no sign of Broadway. "It can't be this far!" I reasoned. "I can't walk back two miles to the University." I panicked, "What am I going to do?" Ahead, I saw a bridge. "If I cross that bridge, I'll really be lost," Quickly, I pulled off the road.

Surveying my surroundings, I realized I'd pulled into a bad area of town. Everything looked greasy and grimy, with graffiti on the walls. Broken cars sat all around me.

"Oh, my, now I've really done it!" I started crying. I cried and cried. Through my tears, I saw a policeman directing traffic behind me. *I'll try and get his attention*, I thought, and I rolled down my window. But I cried so hard, I couldn't call to him.

Just then five people, four men and a woman, walked toward me from behind my car. They passed me. "Oh, well, so they see me cry." Totally embarrassed, I told myself, *Everyone cries now and again. They've seen people cry before, I'm sure.* One man looked my direction. He saw me crying. He motioned for the others to stop. He pointed, "That woman is crying!" They all stopped and stared. They walked toward my car.

One of the men bent toward my open window. "May we help you, ma'am?" he asked.

"I'm lost! Hopelessly lost!" I showed them my map and told them, I'd found the university all right, but hadn't found Broadway Street or the Broadway Parking Garage.

"Come on, fellows, let's just pile in her car and show her where to go."
Coming from a small town, I never keep my car doors locked. They opened
my doors and the four men piled into the back of my little blue Mazda. I
moved my purse from the front seat so the woman could sit in front with me.

"I'm sorry my car is such a mess," I apologized.

"Oh, that's all right," one of them said.

Even though it never occurred to me to be frightened, I remember praying,
"Lord, if You sent them, thanks! If You didn't, protect me!"

"Turn left here," one of the men said.

"Now, turn right," another directed and showed me where to go. After a
few turns, I saw the Broadway Parking Garage. "This is where I belong," I told
them. "Thank you so much." I reached for my purse. "You're a long way from
where I picked you up. What can I pay you to get you back to where you
were?" I asked.

One man said, "We'd appreciate five dollars, ma'am!"

"You've got it!" I said and handed them a five-dollar bill. They clambered
out of my car, went their way, and I went mine. Shaken up, I thought, *How
stupid of me to pick up five strangers!*

The next evening, at home, my husband removed my suitcase from the
back seat. The following morning, I retrieved the half ream of paper with two
master copies lying on top. I wanted the master copies perfect because I
needed them to make flyers. I also removed a gift, towels, and two tissue
boxes from the back seat. I discovered not one paper moved or wrinkled.
The gift and tissue boxes I found undisturbed and uncrushed!

I stopped unloading and asked myself, *Where did those four big men sit back
here? They didn't crush or move a thing!*

Everything appeared perfectly in place, where I had initially put it. I finally realized, "There's no way five big people besides me could fit into my little Mazda. Now I'm positive my unusual passengers were angels sent to help me out of my lost dilemma in that big city."

As told by Christie Forsyth.

White-Robed Repairman

HIS INCIDENT IS AS VIVID in my mind today as though it happened yesterday. When I was five or six years old, I lived with my parents, two older brothers and two younger brothers in an old, two-story country home. We heated this old house with a wood cook stove and a potbellied heater. Father rented the farmland surrounding this house year after year. During spring, summer and fall, we lived in this old house. But in winter we moved to our home in town just three miles away.

One cold autumn day, my two older brothers arose early to help Dad in the field before school began. That left me, the only girl in the family, to play alone in the yard. That was nothing new. I usually played alone.

While I played, suddenly a loud rustle shook the trees surrounding our house. I turned, looked up to see what caused the racket. There on our roof, I saw the most beautiful, white angelic being. He climbed the wooden shingles, straightened the fallen, tin-pipe chimney and anchored the pipe with wires. After he secured the pipe in an upright position, he disappeared quicker than he came.

While he worked, I stood transfixed in amazement. After he left, I excitedly ran into the house shouting, "Mother! Mother! You won't believe what just I saw!"

"What, child?"

"A man dressed in white on our roof," I jumped from one foot to the other ecstatic with excitement. "He straightened our tipped chimney and tightened it with the loose wires."

"Really?" Mother's eyes widened in unbelief.

"If you don't believe me, then come and see for yourself."

"I noticed that fallen chimney yesterday and meant to tell your father about it, but he's been so busy working in the fields from dawn 'til dark."

"Remember, you told us we have guardian angels, Mama!" I insisted. "I just *saw* our guardian angel fix our chimney!"

"Yes, I think you're right, child," Mother said looking at the upright chimney. She could hardly believe her eyes. "Thank You, Lord, for saving our home and, likely, our family from a burning house," Mother prayed aloud as she stared at the anchored chimney.

As told by Juanita Holm.

CHAPTER 20

Bill and the Bull

OME ON, UNCLE BILL," twelve-year-old Wally said. "Let's get a couple of halters and a bucket of oats from the barn. There are several horses in the pasture and if we can catch a couple of them, we can go for a ride."

"Sounds like fun." Turning to his nephew Johnny, fifteen and a year older than he, Bill said, "Sorry you can't come too." Johnny had broken his leg in a recent accident.

On this early, sunny afternoon, Bill eagerly followed Wally to the barn. With two halters and a bucket of oats, they hiked into the thousand-acre pasture, which had no cross-fencing. Four farmers let their horses and cattle feed and run freely in this large area.

Bill found his first visit to his older sister's farm peaceful and relaxing. Even the distant horizon appeared clear of smog and haze. Though a few willow bushes grew along the gully, Bill particularly noticed the absence of shade trees for the animals.

"Here comes a horse! Rattle the bucket, Uncle Bill. After he starts eating, I'll slip the halter over his head." With the halter in place, they looked for a second catch. Suddenly they noticed to one side of the pasture a big, black Angus bull angrily pawing the ground.

"Quick, Uncle Bill, put me on the horse!" Wally shouted. Bill boosted Wally onto the horse and intended to climb on behind him.

"This horse won't carry two," Wally yelled and galloped away.

Panic gripped Bill's whole being! He knew you do not toy with an angry bull that can run more than thirty miles an hour. The bull charged!

Suddenly Bill realized he was still alive—standing in the crook of a tree, six feet above the bulging eyes of the black bull.

Wham! The snorting bull's head hit the tree trunk. The tree quivered! Bill trembled! His knuckles turned white as he gripped the limb. For two hours the dirt-pawing, angry monster kept Bill treed. He changed one aching foot after the other in the cramped tree fork.

"Please help me, Lord!" Bill prayed.

After an eternity, Johnny, despite his injury, rode his horse to rescue Bill. The bull charged Johnny on his horse and would not allow them near Bill's tree sanctuary. In desperation, Johnny herded some cattle past, and the bull joined them.

Trembling and relieved, Bill climbed out of the tree and onto the horse behind Johnny. They rode safely home.

Many times since then, Bill has wondered: *How did I get into that tree's safety? I don't recall climbing it hand over hand. Nor do I remember leaping into the air to catch a branch. When I reached that tree, how far behind me was that snorting Angus? Above all, I've often wondered, where did the tree come from? Yes, where did the tree come from? I hadn't seen any trees around that area before we caught the horse.*

Bill is positive angels were in that pasture to deliver him from the big, angry bull that day. But he still asks, "Where *did* that tree come from?"

As told by Bill Nelson.

CHAPTER 21

Bill and the Bear

S A NINETEEN-YEAR-OLD first-time teacher, I looked forward to the beginning of the school year. Since Wednesday I'd prepared my classroom and lessons. The Chiefswood school board told me to expect about forty-five students grades one through ten. However, the number of student grew to sixty-two as the school year progressed. The large student body didn't discourage me, and I went on to teach for forty-two years after my first year at Chiefswood.

The school was a distance beyond a hamlet of approximately four hundred people. Behind the school and the playground stood a large forest. When Friday evening came, I had everything prepared for Monday.

For a break I explored the path into the forest. I enjoyed the evening shadows, the sounds of dusk, and the poignant odors of poplar and pine trees. As I walked along, I met several horses. Thinking the owner may want them in the barnyard for the night, I stepped aside into the dark forest to let them pass. After they had gone by, I stepped back onto the path to find a man, fifty feet away, with his gun aimed at me.

Startled, I yelled, "What's going on?" Without saying a word, the dazed man lowered his gun and confronted me.

"You're a lucky fellow!" he exclaimed. "Do you see those corrals through the trees?" He pointed. "That's where my wife milks our cows. For the last three nights a black bear came from the forest, disturbing the cows. Tonight, I was determined to get him. When you came out of the dark, I was sure you were the bear! Your shout saved you, young man! With my finger on the trigger, in less than a heartbeat, you would have been dead. You're one lucky fellow!"

"Yes, I am a lucky fellow," I said.

Today, I believe it was more than "luck" that saved me. The God of heaven sent His angel to protect me. Truly "the angel of the Lord encampeth around them that fear Him, and delivereth them" (Psalm 34:7).

As told by Bill Nelson.

CHAPTER 22

In Human Disguise

ORRY, ALL THE BOATS LEFT early today because of an approaching storm," the Bangladeshi coolies told missionaries Brown and Toews.

"Nothing we can do now!" the coolies exclaimed. Coolies are men who carry passenger's luggage to and from boats. People travel everywhere by boat in this country so coolies keep busy all day long.

"What are we going to do?" Pastor Brown asked Mr. Toews.

"I don't know!" Mr. Toews answered, looking up at Pastor Brown. "Now we won't be able to meet our appointments beyond this wide expanse of water." He motioned toward the river. During monsoon season, rivers have no limits, as was the case that day.

As the two men stood on the dock, pondering their next move, out of nowhere a well-dressed, middle-aged man approached them. Generally, the men of Bangladesh are short and slender, but this man appeared stout and shorter than most nationals there.

"Where do you gentlemen want to go?" he asked, smiling up at them.

"Across this water." Pastor Brown pointed. "We're to attend an important meeting over there. We missed the boat since it left earlier than scheduled."

"Follow me." He guided them to a boat much smaller than the passenger cruiser they had missed. "This boat will take you across the water."

"Where did this boat come from, Pastor Brown?" Mr. Toews asked softly.

"I don't know," he whispered. "It was nowhere in sight before," he said, and Mr. Toews agreed. Without hesitation they walked on board. Tickets are usually purchased from the purser on the boat. But this time, the missionaries paid the captain for their tickets. As a rule, boats are always crowded, but soon the missionaries realized they were the only passengers on the boat.

Since darkness began to fall, the captain immediately nosed his boat into calm water. On the top deck, the missionaries spread their sleeping bags behind the wheelhouse and stretched out to rest. Without a storm, they arrived at their destination in time for their scheduled appointments.

To this day, these two missionaries thank and praise God for His help that day. After all, they were on the King's business. They are certain that the well-dressed man, an angel in human disguise, was God-sent. They are certain our Father in heaven also provided the special boat so they could meet their important appointments.

As told by Martha Toews.

CHAPTER 2 3

Angel Deliverance

HE WALTER TOEWS FAMILY had just arrived in Pakistan as new missionaries. Walter, the secretary-treasurer of a mission in Pakistan, and all the mission members were scheduled to attend meetings at mission college, about thirty miles from the mission's office located in the city of Lahore.

"We need to leave in a few minutes," Walter told his wife, Martha.

"We're ready to go," Martha said. "Here, take this suitcase to the car, David."

"Okay, Mom." Her twelve-year-old son grabbed the suitcase, while she carried one-year-old Bruce and hustled to the car.

"This is going to be a special treat for us to get out of the city," Walter said.

"It surely will!" Martha agreed. "I'm looking forward to meeting other missionary families and discussing with them how to meet the challenges of mission life."

The weekend meetings and fellowship went well and concluded at 5:00 P.M. on Sunday.

"Guess it's time we left for the city," Walter announced after a delicious supper at the president's home.

"Walter, I think it would be best if you spend the night with us and leave in the morning," the president suggested. "It's not safe to travel that road at night because of marauding bandits. In the daytime the road is busy with trucks, buses, carts, tongas, bicycles, donkeys, goats, men, women and children. Only trucks and buses travel at night."

"Thank you for inviting us to stay, but I need to be at the office first thing in the morning," Walter insisted and arose from the table. "Let's get the suitcases, Martha and David, and be on our way."

"Okay, Dad." David jumped up to get their things. Martha got baby Bruce ready for their trip home.

After the car was loaded and friendly goodbyes were said, the president and college dean ushered them out the mission compound gate.

At dusk they drove away from the compound and Walter turned on the headlights. "Seems like we have the whole road to ourselves, David," Walter turned to his son beside him in the front seat. After moments of silence, he continued, "Looks like Mom and Bruce are asleep already. They're tired. We've had a busy, but good, weekend. Did you enjoy it, David?"

"Yes, Dad, it was fun and I made some new friends."

As they motored through semi-desert country, they passed high, mud-walled villages scattered here and there.

Suddenly Walter tapped the brakes. The car came to a complete stop.

"What's the problem?" Sleepily, Martha sat up in the back seat and asked, "Do we have a flat tire?"

"There's a barricaded bridge in front of our car," Walter said.

"Oh, dear! That could spell trouble! What shall we do? We could turn around and go back," Martha suggested.

"Let's pray," David said. Anxiously his Dad looked for other vehicles behind or in front of them, but there were none.

"Yes, let's pray," Walter said, "Dear Lord, please give us Your guidance and protection."

"I'll leave the motor running and the lights on," Walter said as he crawled out of the car and began making a passageway through the debris of barrels, wire, rocks, and sticks—probably rigged up by bandits hiding under the bridge.

As Walter pushed and pulled debris to clear the roadway onto the bridge, the entire area lit up.

"Wow! Look at all the lights on the two trucks and bus behind us, Mom!" David shouted.

"Yes, I see, and look in front of us at the other side of the bridge. There are two more trucks and a bus with glaring lights. This reminds me of Israel's Red Sea and Jordan River experiences," Mom told David. "Only when Israel moved forward in faith and put their feet in the water did God work a miracle in their behalf."

"This is great!" David said, "Now Dad will have a lot of help cleaning away that junk."

"Besides, if there are bandits under the bridge, they will hesitate to pick on us now," Martha said, "because each truck has four or five armed men in it."

The Toews were overcome with awe at the sudden change from the lonely darkness to light and the six vehicles behind and in front of them. It all seemed very unusual. They felt surrounded by a heavenly atmosphere.

Walter continued throwing rubbish over the side of the bridge. Surprisingly, no one from any of the vehicles got out to help him. Ordinarily, the Pakistani people would not allow missionaries to do any menial work.

After Walter cleared a passageway, he came back to the car. "This is all so strange!" he said. "I'm going to slowly drive over the bridge and see what happens after we pass the last vehicle."

"The buses are loaded with people," David said as they passed the vehicles on the opposite side of the bridge. "They're looking through their windows at us. They are all dressed in white!" he exclaimed. "Look, Mom, they're not natives either!"

Immediately after they passed the last vehicle, they were alone. Only their headlights remained to pierce the dark, shadowy night. No other headlights ever followed them that night.

All the way home, their hearts overflowed with gratitude to their Heavenly Father for sending a "legion" of angels to protect them from the bandits. Even today, whenever they think of this experience, they thank God for His great love and protection that lonely night in Pakistan.

As told by Martha Toews.

CHAPTER 24

More Than Mush

NNIE FROWNED AT THE SUPPER TABLE. Inwardly she stamped her foot. "Again, Mama!"

"Yes, daughter. Mush again. Come now, sit down and be glad for it. Our stomach walls would touch if we didn't have mush."

Annie pinched her lips tight, sat down, and wondered about God. After supper, the mush sat like a cold stone in Annie's stomach. They gathered around Pa for worship. Annie usually loved Pa's quiet deep tones as he read. His calm trust usually comforted her. But tonight Annie wanted something more.

"Although the field yields not her fruit . . . yet will I rejoice," Pa read.

"Pa," Annie said, "does that mean we'll be glad even if there's nothin' but mush to eat?"

"That's right, daughter." Pa smiled at her.

"Well, I like what David said better, Pa."

"What's that, child? Show me."

Annie found the place in the old family Bible and pointed, "Let's see, Psalm 81, verse 10." A slow smile crossed Pa's face as he read, "Open your mouth wide, and I will fill it."

"He's done that, hasn't He? Filled our mouths with mush," Marian, Annie's older sister, said with a little laugh.

"David didn't mean mush, Marian!" Annie said with sharp irritation.

Later, in bed, Annie couldn't sleep. She turned onto her side, thinking about God and mush. Surely God loved her more than to give just hateful, old mush, didn't He? Pa talked about a mysterious stock market fall. The long drought caused job losses and food shortages.

"Why did God let it happen?" Annie wondered aloud.

Restless, she got up and looked out her bedroom window. From her tiny room above the kitchen, she saw flat, dry ground that stretched to forever. The dry, dusty eastern Oregon ranchlands cracked from lack of water. Soon the sky, alive with twinkles, caught Annie's attention. She stared at the silver-spangled blackness and mulled over what Ma often repeated these days:

"Trust grows in sunshine, but what's best—it blooms in darkness, when at rest."

"Okay," Annie told God. "I'll go along with Ma and Pa and old Marian too. "Maybe You know something I don't. I'll try to trust You more. I'll even try to like mush a little bit." Annie stretched out on top of the quilts and drifted into a deep sleep.

Scraa-aape. Scraa-aatch!

The strange sound awakened Annie. Drowsily, she heard the screen door slam and Pa's voice, "Git gone, Bossie! Go along, now."

Wondering, Annie jumped up and pushed aside the curtains. "A cow!" she shouted. A large yellow-brown Jersey splashed with black as though someone had paint-splattered her trotted toward the road.

Annie stretched and pulled on her clothes when she heard the strange scraping again. She looked down and saw the same cow rubbing her horns against the porch post. The screen door slammed. Pa stepped onto the porch.

This time he briskly slapped his pants with his hand. The startled cow shook her head and ran down the path. Her udder, swollen with milk, swung back and forth as she trotted.

Minutes later, Annie joined Marian and her parents in the kitchen. "Where'd that cow come from, Pa?" Annie asked.

"I imagine she belongs to some rancher 'round here, Annie. 'Cause of the draught, they've turned their stock loose to forage for themselves. Poor critters." He shook his head sympathetically. Just then the scraping returned.

They went out to the porch and stared at the big bovine. She stared back dully; then lifting her head, she drew out a long, sad *Moo*.

"Pa, she wants to be milked. Look at her full udder," Marian said. She took a step toward the Jersey, then stopped as the animal swung her head, brandishing sharp horns. Her hoofed foot stamped the dust, raising swirls from the parched ground.

"Hey, I'll milk her! Then we'll have cream on our mush, won't that be good?" Annie said and looked appealingly at Pa. "Can I, Pa? Please. She's come here, asking."

"Annie, part of her looks like she wants to be milked, all right. But her horns and that look in her eye say no one better bother her."

"Let me try, Pa. Please. If she doesn't want me to, she'll just leave."

"All right, child. Go ahead and try, but I don't think she'll even let you near her."

Annie slipped into the kitchen and grabbed a large kettle. Carrying it, she walked slowly toward the tail-switching cow. A front hoof pawed at the dusty ground. Annie hesitated, her breath caught in her throat. That cow really didn't look too friendly. Then she thought, *Cream on our mush. I'll bet this cow is from God.*

She took another slow step. "There now, little mama," she said softly. "We'll soon have you feeling better." With slow, steady movements Annie positioned the kettle. Within minutes streams of rich, warm milk filled it to the brim.

Just as Annie finished, the cow flung her head and ran. Sharp hoofs barely missed the kettle.

"Wow!" Marian breathed. "Annie, you were brave. I think she isn't too tame."

"Let's go have our mush with milk, Marian."

As Pa said the blessing, Annie felt tongue-tied. Inside, she added her silent Thank You to God.

Early next morning, as sleepy bird songs began, Annie's dreams were shattered by the familiar scraping sound.

"Oh! You've sent her again, God?" Annie drew in a quick breath. She flew downstairs, snatched the kettle and raced outdoors.

"Oh, Bossie dear, I'm so glad you came back. We loved the milk you gave us yesterday. Do you belong to God, Bossie?" Talking gently, Annie soon filled the pan with Bossie's creamy milk.

Each morning throughout the hot, dry summer, the cow returned and Annie's young, strong fingers milked her. Mama said she could give the cow a bucket of precious water as part payment for her milk.

Days grew shorter and cooler. Finally one day a long, drenching downpour sank deep into the thirsty ground. Soon Pa found work and bought food once more.

One morning a rancher rode up to the door. "Good mornin', Ma'am," he said to Mama. "I'm rounding up my cattle I turned loose earlier. There's one I'm missin'—a Jersey, a big 'un with black on one side. Wonder if you've seen her?"

"Oh my, yes!" Mama said. "Is she yours? We've wondered who she belongs to. She's been coming every morning for months. My Annie's been milking her and—"

"Nope, not her then, Ma'am," he interrupted. "This 'un wouldn't let a husky man milk her, let alone a tad of a girl. Mean, she is," he said with a scowl.

"Well, this cow's skittish, all right. But she apparently lost her calf and was heavy with milk, so each day she came and Annie milked her. And she does have black on one side."

"Naw, I just can't glimmer her being milked by a little girl. Still, you say one side's got black? Maybe I'll drop by in the mornin' and have a look."

"Well, I'll be switched! That's my Jersey—sure as can be." The rancher said the next morning as he slowly walked around the cow while Annie milked her. "Yep, there's my brand, all right. But say, little girl. You're doing something no youngster's ever done."

After Annie finished milking, he led the cow down the road. Annie watched her go. Deep inside she smiled at God and said, *Thanks, God, for filling our mouths with more than mush—creamy milk from Your cow!*

Written by Jeanine Bartling.
First published in Friend, *May 1987. Used by permission.*

CHAPTER 25

Help's on the Way

 UESS IT'S TIME TO START TRUCKING," Ken told his parents as they relaxed on the living room couch. He lived with his wife and children in Fallon, Nevada—but only on weekends. Monday through Thursday he worked ten hours a day in a gold mine about fifty miles from home. Ken treasured weekend visits with his family, who lived in town because their children attended school. A foreman at the mine, father lived with mother in a mobile home near the mine. Ken boarded with his folks during the week.

"Did you look out and see the snow?" his mother asked after she arose, moved the curtain, and peered through the dusk outdoors. "It's falling thick and fast, Ken. There's a lot of snow to plow through. Are you sure we should leave this evening?"

"With our four-wheel-drive pickup we should make it okay," Ken said. "If we hadn't promised to meet the boss, we could leave Sunday morning instead of tonight."

"If we move along carefully, we should make it all right," Dad added. "Let's get our things ready and shove off before it gets late."

The 1969-1970 winter proved challenging for Nevada miners. Deep snow made travel difficult. Fresh snow fell daily.

As Ken and his parents backed out of his driveway, they found falling snow like a lace curtain blocking their headlights. Their bumper slowly pushed through dry powder. A strong wind whistled and the temperature continued to drop.

"Not the best time to go for an evening drive," Ken broke the silence. Soon they turned off the pavement and crept along a country "pole-line" road.

Clunk! The motor purred but the wheels quit turning. The truck slowed to a stop. The drive shaft had broken between the transfer case and transmission. Stranded in the desert, miles from farms or Indian homes, they pulled on extra clothes and struggled into sleeping bags. All night the three of them squirmed and tossed in the truck cab, while the temperature plunged to twenty degrees below zero.

After the most miserable night of their lives, Sunday morning dawned cloudless. For miles all they could see was a continuous white landscape that met the blue sky. The hills of their destination, like scoops of ice cream, sat about twenty-five miles distant.

"There's only one thing for me to do," Ken told his folks. "I'd best hike across Ione Valley to the main road. Maybe I can get some help."

"I'll go with you," Dad insisted.

"No, Dad. I think you'd best stay here with Mother." Ken crunched a frozen sandwich. "You've got food and water. Stay in the truck and keep warm the best you can." Dad, not in the best of health, finally agreed to stay with Mother.

"We'll be praying for you, Ken," Mother said. Ken crawled from the truck. Frigid air gripped his lungs. At sunrise, he hiked on top of frozen snow and made good time. As the sun warmed, the frozen crust softened. With each struggling step, Ken's feet sank deeper and deeper. Soon he sank to mid-thigh with each move and progress became slow.

Dark clouds tumbled across the sky, obscuring the sun and distant hills. Snow fell thick and fast.

Meanwhile at the truck, his parents worried. "I should go after Ken and see if he made it to the highway," Dad told Mother.

"Please stay here with me," she pled. "Let's pray and ask God to give us a sign. If the sun comes out at noon we'll know Ken's safe."

"All right," Dad reluctantly agreed and prayed, "Please keep Ken from harm and give us the sign we agreed upon as reassurance that he's all right." Just before noon the sun broke through the clouds for five minutes. They knew God had heard their prayer and Ken was safe.

Finally Ken pulled his exhausted body onto the county road. During the winter, probably one car a week would use this road. He did not see the sun. Puffing, he collapsed on the snow to rest. "Thank You, Lord, for giving me strength to come this far. I have a long way to go and I desperately need help."

In the desert everything is extremely quiet and one can hear a sound for miles, but Ken heard nothing. Somewhat rested, he struggled to his feet and began walking toward the mine—still ten to fifteen miles away. About twenty steps later, he heard a motor. He turned and saw a white Ford pickup come over the rise behind him.

"This is the most beautiful sight," he said aloud as the pickup stopped. The driver rolled down his window.

"What are you two men doing out here in this storm?" Ken asked the strangers.

"We're looking for lost sheep," the Basque sheepherders told him.

"You've just found one," Ken said, wondering why they'd be looking for white sheep in a white snowstorm. Sheep would never survive in the deep snow. Besides, Dad had lived in this country since 1936 and had never seen a flock of sheep.

"Get in," the driver said. "Where are you going?" he asked.

"To the mine," Ken pointed and told the men about his broken truck. He observed the men dressed in neat, clean jeans. They did not use bad language. Nor did the truck smell of smoke.

"The warmth of your truck feels good," Ken told them. "I hope my folks didn't freeze to death in my stranded pickup."

When they arrived at the fork in the road, two miles from the mine, Ken told them, "You may let me off here and I can walk the last couple of miles."

"No, we'll take you up there," they insisted. Halfway up the mountain, they met the mine owner's vehicle and stopped.

"Thank you for the ride!" Ken told his new friends. "You saved my life." As Ken walked to his boss's truck, the white pickup turned around and left.

"My truck broke down on the way over here last evening," Ken told his boss and explained where his truck was stranded. They followed the tracks of the white pick-up since it traveled the way Ken's boss planned to go. The white Ford broke trail right to Ken's stranded truck.

The men in the white truck had stopped beside Ken's truck and told his parents, "Help is on the way." After the men rolled up their window and drove down the road, no one ever saw them or the white Ford pickup again. God's providence surpasses all other! Ken and his parents are certain that the two men were angels sent to help them.

As told by Kenneth Silver.

CHAPTER 26

The Mystery Cookie

MID THE CHRISTMAS RUSH, I set aside one morning to bake cookies. Hurriedly, I ground walnuts with my hand grinder. This grinder consists of a plastic upper cup, an outer handle, and a main shaft with twelve metal prongs inside the cup. The cup screws onto a glass container.

Suddenly, as I ground the walnuts, the handle turned with difficulty. *Crack!* *Crunch!* Certain I had demolished a sturdy walnut shell, I stopped, unscrewed the lid, poured out the nuts, and picked out the shells.

My mother always told me, "Haste makes waste!" I lost precious moments looking for bits of shell. *Had I checked the nuts before putting them into the grinder, this would not have happened,* I thought to myself. Quickly, I replaced the cup and finished the job. The first five dozen chocolate chip cookies, our family's favorites, looked delicious as they cooled.

Pleased that I reached my baking goal that morning, I washed the utensils, when horror struck me! I turned weak! I couldn't believe my eyes. Checking the shaft in my grinder a second time, I found a one-quarter inch metal prong missing! All the prongs were intact before I began grinding, I was sure. That tough shell broke the metal prong! "Why didn't I find the prong when I sorted out the shells?" I asked myself.

Gazing at the cookies, I considered throwing them out and making a fresh batch. How could I risk sharing Christmas cookie plates with neighbors and friends? Certainly, I did not want our grandchildren or anyone else to bite into a cookie and break a tooth on that metal prong. I debated. The safest way would be to throw them all out, but "Waste not, want not," drilled into me by my frugal, Depression-surviving mother, nagged me.

"Lord," I prayed, "You know which cookie contains that metal prong. You know I don't want anyone to break a tooth, cut a cheek, or swallow it. Neither do I want to waste my time and ingredients by throwing them away. Please, let *me* be the one to get that mystery cookie. Thank You for hearing my prayer."

The next Sunday our three-year-old and four-year-old granddaughters came to spend the morning and have lunch with us. They always looked forward to lunch at Grandpa's and Grandma's house—especially dessert. Hesitantly, I put some chocolate chip cookies on the table.

"Yummy!" Our three-year-old's dimpled hand reached for the cookie with the most chocolate chips. "I love 'tocolate!" she said, selecting a chip-loaded cookie.

Our four-year-old said, "I want the biggest one!" and reached for her choice.

While Grandpa chose the next cookie, I scarcely breathed. Then I prayed again, "Lord, please save the cookie with the metal prong for *me!*"

While the children and Grandpa enjoyed their cookies, I chose one. The first few bites proved all right. Then *crunch!* I chomped on something hard, positive that I had broken my left molar! Thinking I had missed a nutshell, I took a hard object from my mouth. I found not a shell but the missing metal prong!

"Thank You, Lord, for saving the mystery cookie for me." I silently prayed. I showed the metal prong to Grandpa and the children and shared my story.

This story happened several Christmases ago. Each time I finish chopping nuts with that little grinder, the missing prong reminds me of this faith-boosting incident and loving heavenly Father who cares even about little things.

Published in He's Alive, *November/December 1996.*

CHAPTER 27

The Miracle Hose

QUIET PEACE PERVADED our little cottage beside the placid lake. Quietly and quickly the sun slipped beneath the horizon. Darkness settled over the cove. Inside the cottage lived a family of four—Bill, Kathy, and two lovely four and six-year-old daughters, Evie and Kristy.

"One more story—please, Grammy," Kristy pleaded. Their Grammy had come to visit and the girls loved Grammy's bedtime stories.

"It's time," their mother, Kathy, reminded them with her I-mean-business look. "Time to say prayers and hop into bed."

That night Evie asked to pray. "Dear Jesus, keep us safe. I love you—and dear God, come pick us up soon. Amen." After the children were tucked into bed and said their "goodnights," they soon slept. Kathy and Grammy hurried downstairs to complete their last task before retiring.

In spite of the frosty October nights, the wood stove had cooled all day because ashes needed to be removed. "There's a few ashes left in the heater," Kathy said, handing a paper bag to Grammy.

"Would you please clean out the last of them, Mother?"

"I'll be glad to." With bare hands, Grammy scooped cold ashes into the paper bag and set the bag in the garage. Exhausted, they went to bed. Soon sleep and silence enveloped the cottage.

Suddenly, Kathy awoke. She felt a nudge and a voice whisper, "Go check the back door." She glanced at the clock—nearly 2:00 A.M. Automatically she arose, slipped downstairs and tip-toed to the back door. Realizing how exhausted she felt, she thought, *This is nuts! No reason to go to the back door— maybe the front door. No, I'm too tired,* she told herself, turned and headed upstairs.

Again, an unseen hand—urgent this time—turned her back toward the garage door. "Check the back door *now!*" The commanding, but quiet voice urged. This time she didn't argue. She swung open the back door. Orange flames leaped and danced towards her. Thick, black smoke filled the entire garage.

Horrified, she screamed, "Fire, Bill, Fire!" In a flash, Bill jumped out of bed and tore into the icy-cold night to extinguish the blaze. Grammy dashed to the phone to call the fire department. The phone was dead!

Black smoke billowed up the stairs after Kathy. She raced to carry her precious girls to safety. The extreme fatigue, which previously haunted her, had fled. She pulled the girls with their blankets from warm beds, tore downstairs, and placed them on the floor near the front door. There, away from danger, Grammy comforted her granddaughters' sobs and panic.

Oblivious to the icy night air, Kathy ran outdoors in her nightgown to help Bill put out the fire. She dashed for a hose.

"Pull on that hose," her husband demanded. The hose, lying in a pipe under a large cement slab, wouldn't budge. She pulled and pulled in the darkness and felt a junction in the hose. Quickly, she unscrewed it, dashed to the burning garage, and aimed the hose at the flames. No water!

"God, give me water!" Kathy prayed aloud. Instantly, water gushed. What seemed like forever, she extinguished one flame after another until the fire appeared under control. She dropped the hose and left Bill to assess the smoldering mess.

When she hurried to the front door, Kathy found Grammy and her sobbing girls still huddled in their blankets. "I think the fire is under control now," she hugged them reassuringly. She loaded them into the Blazer and drove to loving neighbors for safekeeping and help.

As she drove back to the cottage, she prayed, "Lord, I know You give good gifts in every situation, but right now, I don't understand what's good in this mess. Show me, Lord!"

Back at the cottage, Kathy surveyed the situation. She noticed eerie, black, smoldering images sitting outside the water-soaked garage. Suddenly a folded-up hide-a-bed broke into flames. Bill grabbed the hose and directed it toward the burning bed. No water!

"Turn on the hose, Kathy," he yelled. Obediently she opened the faucet and waited. No water flowed. Bill checked it for kinks—no kinks! "Why, no water?" They both wondered. Bill threw the hose on the wet cement. A small dribble came—then stopped. The hose was frozen! They twisted, pounded, and bent the hose. No water! Occasionally, it spit ice chunks, then clogged again.

"Kathy, how did you get water to put out the fire?" Bill asked as they snatched buckets, ran to the lake for water, and extinguished the rekindled bed.

"I thought you turned on the tap," Kathy responded.

"No, I didn't. I thought you did," he said. "You mean you got all that water and the tap wasn't even turned on?"

Then the truth dawned! She realized what had really happened. "Wow, Lord," she prayed. "Thanks for being our Water of Life tonight! You are awesome!"

Written by Kathy Hendrixson,
revised by Nathalie Ladner-Bischoff.

C H A P T E R   2 8

Intercessory Prayer

FTER A LONG FLIGHT from Anchorage, Alaska, in July, Clayton and Darlene stepped off the plane at 5:30 A.M. They found their luggage, loaded it into their car, which they'd parked at the airport two weeks earlier, and started for home across the state of Washington.

Fourteen days they worked hard with sixty other volunteers at Wasilla, near Anchorage, constructing a new church for the members there. Extremely fatigued, they eagerly sped on I-90, and other routes diagonally across Washington to the southeastern corner—home!

Fighting drowsiness, they alternated driving and sleeping. After a breakfast stop, and on the road again, Clayton said, "You'd better drive, Darlene. I'm too sleepy."

Darlene drove from Ellensburg to Wapato while Clayton slept. In Prosser, they visited Darlene's brother. Again, in Kennewick they shopped and ate lunch. Clayton took the wheel for the final stretch, when sleep overpowered him. He glanced at Darlene—sound asleep. He didn't have the heart to awaken her and ask her to drive. He fought to stay awake.

Shortly after 3:00 P.M., they entered Touchet, about fifteen miles from home. Clayton dozed, crossed the yellow line, and missed a U-Haul truck. However, their car's front wheel hit the wheels of the trailer the truck pulled, carrying a small car, and blew the wheels to pieces. What a horrible noise! It woke Darlene up. Next, the car, still free, headed for another car—head-on. The other car swerved one way, Clayton the other. The cars missed each other, and Clayton and Darlene stopped—unhurt. The impact took a chunk out of Clayton's tire, so he changed the tire and walked back to the U-Haul truck.

He found the lone truck driver, a lady from West Virginia, on her way to Eugene, Oregon, shook-up but unhurt. Clayton told her, "Don't worry about this. I'll take care of it for you."

At home, Clayton called the local U-Haul office and reported the accident. He asked them to deliver another trailer to Touchet and reload the little car. Within two hours, the lady was on her way.

From the pulpit on Sabbath, the pastor acknowledged the near-tragedy, saying, "We're thankful that Clayton and Darlene weren't hurt in an accident this past week."

After church, Cindy, also a volunteer of the church-building team who'd flown to Seattle from Alaska, but who had taken an alternate route home through Portland, Oregon, asked Darlene, "Did you have an accident?"

"Yes, we had an accident." Darlene told her.

"Do you know while I shopped in Portland, suddenly, I felt a strong anxiety about you folks driving alone. I couldn't shake that anxious feeling until I prayed, 'Dear Lord, Clayton and Darlene are very tired and driving alone. Please watch over them.' The Holy Spirit impressed me to pray for you, I'm sure."

"Cindy, what time did you do that?" Darlene asked.

"Just a few minutes before 3:00 P.M." Cindy said.

"The accident happened a few minutes after 3:00 P.M. Thank you for your prayer, Cindy," Darlene told her. "I'm sure that's why we're in church today."

As told by Darlene Prusia.
Published by The Gleaner, *December 11, 1995.*

CHAPTER 29

God's Fragrant Providences

❧

GOD SAYS WE'RE TO ACCEPT EVERYBODY! That means, you're supposed to love my girlfriend!" my husband shouted. "Why can't you accept two women in a marriage?"

"Because I can't," I told him and we divorced. I really struggled with religion after my husband threw that at me. I even put the Bible away for a while because it was too painful. "I know You're far more powerful than a little black book," I told God. "I know You show me Your love in Your own way."

Divorce brought drastic changes into my life. I lost a lot of church friends. Most likely, divorce frightened them. Then I became turned off on religious things, because my church didn't want anything to do with me. As a single mother, with two children, I struggled on the poverty level for four years. But through it all, I attempted to maintain some sanity and decency.

Even the counselor who dealt with me at one time played the devil's advocate. He said, "Everyone has left you—even God."

"No! No! God's the One thing I have," I insisted when he kept pushing me with that idea. "You can say all you want, but God is all I have right now."

Later, at the end of a session, he said, "You don't know how fortunate you are to know God deep down in every part of your fiber and soul. That's going to take you a long way."

At first, extreme anger overwhelmed me. Especially when I found, hidden under the bed, many religious books and religious dictionaries, as well as pornographic posters which my husband and friend had exchanged. But finally, I understood, God had given me anger in this situation to help me realize something was wrong. I decided to direct my anger in a healthful way to change my life, and I did change it.

"This trouble and pain isn't from God," I reasoned. "It can't be!" Through the next few years, I learned religious interpretation is not as important as a relationship with God. Soon I realized how much He protected me and provided for us.

For example, one weekend, while the children visited their dad, I discovered I was out of everything—one box of tissue left and completely out of toilet paper. Then the phone rang.

"May we come see you?" A friend who'd known me since I was a baby called from Denver. She had no clue I was going through a divorce.

"Yes, of course," I said.

After they arrived, she said, "I hope you don't mind, but I brought you something." They unloaded their station wagon of flour, sugar, bread, tissue, and even a large package of toilet paper—all the necessities I desperately needed.

When the children arrived home and saw all the things, they said, "Mom, I thought you didn't have any money!"

"I don't," I told them. "But God provided." The children and I kept trying, and our communication improved. We struggled to survive. I saw my children learn the lesson that no matter what—God provides!

Traditionally, I allowed each child to buy one new outfit at the beginning of each school year. One day, I called their father and asked, "Could I have forty dollars to help get the children school clothes? All I have is forty dollars for one outfit and I need forty more for the other outfit."

"I give you enough money," he said and hung up.

"Dear God," I prayed, "Maybe You can somehow help me fulfill my tradition and get the children their much-needed school clothes."

That same afternoon, an acquaintance stopped by. Perhaps in a hurry, she didn't come into the house, but asked, "How are you doing, Jeanie?"

"Hangin' in there," I told her.

"Thought I'd stop by and say, Hi." She reached over, took my hand, put something in it, and closed my hand. "Call if you need anything," she said and left. I opened my hand and found forty dollars!

At another time, one October morning, I went out to feed the dogs. There at the corner of the dog pen, I saw a huge lilac branch in full bloom. I love lilacs and had a row of forty or fifty bushes.

Someone must have tied blossoms onto my lilac bush for a joke, I thought. *They can't be blooming this time of year.* The lilacs froze during early spring that year and hadn't bloomed. I strode over to the bush and looked at it—it was attached. I smelled it—it smelled like a lilac.

"It's real!" Looking into the faces of those tiny purple flowers, I felt an incredible peace come over me and melt my heart. The words "Jeanie, things will get better" came to mind. The sight of those fragrant blossoms promised better things ahead and brought more peace into my heart than I'd felt in a long time.

I called a farm neighbor. "You'll never believe this," I told her. "I have a lilac blooming."

"That can't be," she said. "You're mistaken!"

"Come see for yourself," I told her. "I don't lie." She came over to see it because she didn't believe me.

"I don't understand this!" she exclaimed.

"I understand it." I said. "It's a promise to me that things are going to be better in my life." Within a month, I met my present, loving, caring husband. Truly, God provides.

As told by Jean Burgess.

Miracle of Our Lives

RIOR TO THE HISTORICAL BLOOD BATH in Indonesia, my husband, Dr. Jess Holm, our children, and I served as medical missionaries in Bandung, West Indonesia. Our children took home study correspondence courses and were at home during the time of this story.

One Thursday afternoon, Doctor came bounding into the house from work at the hospital. He announced, "Come on kids, let's go to Djakarta today!" Our family had a musical commitment for the opening night of an evangelistic meeting in Djakarta. We planned to leave Friday morning, because Doctor's work took priority.

Baffled at his sudden change of plans, I said, "Quickly, kids, get your bags packed and let's go!" We left Bandung, a mountain city, for the capital, Djakarta, a port city, that Thursday afternoon. We enjoyed the lush green mountains as we drove and stayed at the mission headquarters' guest home. We looked forward to spending the weekend with two missionary families. Our host friends invited us to join them for a Sabbath boat cruise to nearby islands. We looked forward to the cruise and relaxation in God's beautiful nature.

But Friday morning, someone from the embassy called and said, "We understand Dr. Holm is in Djakarta. Is that right?"

"Yes, he's right here. Would you like to speak to him?"

"Please!" the caller from the embassy said. Dr. Holm took the phone.

"What's going on in Bandung, Doctor?"

"I don't know," Doctor said. "But I'll call the hospital and find out what's going on."

"No, Doctor, I don't think you will, because the phone lines are down." He continued, "Since early this morning we've tried to call embassy personnel in Bandung and can't get through. The only way to get through is by short-wave radio." Later, we learned that a horrendous riot had begun in Bandung. Communist rebels destroyed foreigners' property. Their main target was rich Chinese businessmen. The rebels stormed the Chinese shops, destroying imported jewelry and other foreign-made items.

"The things that we can't do anything about, we won't worry about," Doctor told us after he got off the phone. "Let's enjoy the weekend." We did.

After our musical obligation at the evangelistic meeting Sunday evening, we climbed into our car and sped homeward, because Doctor had to work early Monday morning. Just outside Djakarta, near the presidential palaces, a military patrol stopped us.

"The roads are closed to Bandung tonight," the patrol said.

"May I go by your checkpoint here?" Doctor asked.

"I guess so," he said, and we drove 100 kilometers toward the mountains. At the summit, another checkpoint patrolman stopped us.

"Doctor, you cannot go to Bandung," the patrolman, a former patient, told us. "I advise you to stay in one of those little huts for the night."

"I really need to get closer to Bandung tonight," Doctor told him. "May I pass your checkpoint?"

"Well, I guess so," he reluctantly replied, and Doctor maneuvered our car around the checkpoint. Near Bandung, we encountered a third checkpoint. There we repeated the same dialogue. Arriving at Bandung's outskirts, we met a barricade of machine guns and tanks. A soldier walked toward our car.

"There's a curfew in the city," he said. "I cannot let you go in!"

"I'd like to use the telephone," Doctor said.

"There isn't a phone here," he snapped.

"Oh, yes, there is," Doctor said, pointing. "Right over there." In this suburb of Bandung, Doctor had patients who worked at the police station. From the police station, he phoned the General's Assistant, a friend and former patient, and told him, "I'm tired and would like to go home and go to bed."

"Let me talk to the military guard," the assistant said. He told the guard, "Please give Dr. Holm a pass so he can get home and go to bed."

As we drove through Bandung, we strained our eyes to see what the rebels had done. We saw an overturned car and black graffiti scrawled on the white fence surrounding the British Library. In the dark of night, we did not see our Chinese neighbor's tile roof destroyed by rocks.

Once at home, we didn't understand why, but we found a large banner across our front door. It read, "This property is protected by the Indonesian government." We walked in and went to bed.

The next morning, our servants Atjah and Itjah came as they did every morning, and told us the rebel mob started the riot Thursday night and came to our home three times on Friday, while we safely enjoyed our visit in Djakarta. Our servants also told us that a number of Chinese merchants who had helped financially build our hospital came to our home and wanted us to protect their gold, silver, and expensive cars. We found our garage filled with foreign automobiles. Our mission hospital compound housed many other cars behind locked gates for safekeeping. They brought their gold, jewels, and valuables to our hospital's safe. The General had sent guards to protect our mission hospital and our home. Neither suffered damage.

Had we been home during the time of the riot, we would have had to face the rebels and make a decision between the Chinese, who sought our help, and the destructive mob. God spared us by impressing Dr. Holm to leave town before the riot began.

"This is the miracle of our lives, if I ever saw one!" Dr. Holm exclaimed. "God took us out of Bandung just before the riots began and saved us from making critical decisions and untold danger."

As told by Juanita Holm.

CHAPTER 31

Angels in the Blizzard

T 11:00 P.M., I LEFT Pendleton State Hospital, where I worked as a nurse. I opened the door to the warm medical unit and faced the freezing January night. Sleet pelted my face. I raced to my car, cleaned icy snow from the windows, and started the motor. Twenty-five miles seemed like a long road home in the blizzard. For twenty miles, I crept along. Five miles from home a complete whiteout engulfed me. The roadway disappeared. I inched my way, not knowing where the edge of the road hid. Then I hit the right shoulder of the highway.

Suddenly, I felt my car nose downward. Stranded, near midnight, with the front end in the ditch and the back wheels on the shoulder, I prayed, "Lord, please get me out of this ditch." Shoving the gears into reverse, I tried backing onto the road. No success. I bowed my head and prayed again.

Tap, tap! I heard on my window. Turning, I saw the heavenly eyes of a kind-looking man shining a flashlight in at me. Even though the wind howled and sleet peppered him, he appeared perfectly comfortable without hat or gloves and only his beige, linen-weight jacket, open at the neck. The snow didn't even rest on his hair.

"Don't worry. You'll be out of here in a few minutes," he assured me, after I'd rolled down my window. "I'll get the two men in the pickup to pull your car onto the road," he told me and walked back to help the men attach a chain to my car's bumper. Then he came back to my window, saying, "We're ready to pull you out now." I steered, as their truck eased my car onto the highway headed toward home.

The kind man walked back to my car and told me, "You're all clear now. You may go on your way."

"Thank you so much. I can't tell you how grateful I am for your help," and handed him two twenty-dollar bills.

"Oh, no, I don't need that at all," he said, holding up his hand.

"Take it to the men in the pickup," I urged.

"They don't need it either!" he said, walking backward and melting into the blizzard. The pickup's headlights didn't pierce the darkness. I didn't see it pass me or hear a motor go the opposite direction.

Were the helpful gentlemen my guardian angels? I asked myself as I snail-paced homeward. Finally, safe at home, I knelt and thanked God for sending me help in the blizzard. In Hebrews 13:5, He's promised, "I will never leave thee nor forsake thee."

As told by Elsie Jones.

CHAPTER 3 2

Do You Want to Go to Heaven?

HIS INCIDENT TOOK PLACE IN 1924. I was seventeen, almost eighteen. My father and mother, new converts, eagerly attended church each week. As usual, one spring morning I took my parents to church. I attended the youth Sabbath school class a few times and enjoyed it all right. I liked the young people in the class, but I didn't want to attend the church services. The sermons seemed long and boring for me.

I slipped outdoors and sauntered to the car. "I can sleep just as well out in the car as in church," I told myself. Many times in the past, I'd waited for my parents in the car. It seemed a habit by this time. The sunny March day made me drowsy. Soon I dozed. Suddenly a little breeze through the open window startled me. I awoke, and sat upright! I looked up and saw a tall man in an all-white suit approaching the car. He stopped at my window and said, "Young man, do you want to go to heaven?"

"Yes, I do," I replied.

Pointing toward the church, he said, "If you really want to go to heaven, you'd better be in there. Only those inside the church will possibly make it to heaven."

At that instant, I heard a noise rustle the nearby bushes and looked away for just a second. When I turned to face the white-suited stranger, he was gone. I jumped out and walked around our car, but he was nowhere in sight. I walked through the parking lot but couldn't find him among the other cars. I raced around the church but the stranger had obviously vanished. I entered the church and couldn't find a trace of him inside.

That night I had a dream. In my dream, I saw my professor, classmates, and me standing on a hill. All gazed upward. I also looked up and saw Jesus coming in the clouds. Everyone rose off the ground to meet Jesus. That is, everyone but me. I remained on the ground watching.

"Stop! Stop!" I shouted. "Wait for me. I want to go, too!" I awoke in tears! I knelt beside my bed and vowed to God, "I want to be ready to go home with You when You come to take the faithful ones to heaven. I want to live with You forever." That dream left a life-long impression on me. From that day on, I found myself in church every week whenever possible.

As told to Phillip A. Miller of Battle Ground, Washington,
by Melvin J. Powell, who has since passed away.

CHAPTER 33

An Angel in White

OUR YEARS AGO when I was diagnosed with cancer, I was immediately admitted to the hospital for surgery. Tests were taken to determine if the cancer had spread throughout my body, and it was then determined that I had a growth in my liver.

"We cannot tell for sure what it is," Dr. Larry said, "but now that we have found this, we will be better prepared for surgery."

Never had I known such fear. I had previously lost a sister to cancer, and I asked the Lord if this was to be my fate. I prayed as never before, and cried a lot of tears. I prayed for peace of mind more than anything.

The surgery was a grueling six hours. Patiently my family waited for word from the surgeon as to my condition, and eventually they were relieved to hear that the surgery had gone well. As is true with most cancers, the surgeons were not sure that all of it had been removed, but they were ninety percent sure that it wouldn't return.

"The liver had an aneurysm in it and it was the size of a small cantaloupe," the surgeon told my family. "It is not cancerous, but sixty percent of her liver had to be removed."

While my family had received this news, I had no idea as to my condition when I awoke in ICU. Even though I was groggy, I prayed for God to keep me from any more cancer problems.

It was early the next morning when Dr. Larry came to see me. His face beaming, he said, "I just want to tell you that you don't have cancer. I knew you were concerned so I wanted to keep you informed." Only then did I enjoy a peaceful sleep.

The next time I saw Dr. Larry, I was more coherent and realized that I hadn't thanked him for his good news.

"I so want to tell you thanks for letting me know that the liver didn't have any cancer in it," I said. "I appreciated your dropping by."

"I didn't come by," he said, surprised. "This is my first visit since surgery."

"Who told me that then?" I questioned.

"I don't know, but it wasn't me," he assured me before he left.

I figured that with my heavy sedation I had gotten the doctors mixed up, and that it was probably Dr. Little who had given me the news. That evening when Dr. Little stopped by to check on my diabetes, I thanked him for giving me the good news concerning my cancer-free liver.

"It wasn't me!" he exclaimed. "It isn't my place to give you that kind of news. It is Dr. Larry's."

Knowing there were no other doctors involved with my case, I then realized who my early-morning visitor must have been. The face full of compassion and tenderness was that of an angel. Surely Jesus had reached out to me in my sadness and despair and had given me the hope I needed at a critical time.

By Marva Swanson, as told to Charlotte Robinson.
Published by He's Alive, *November/December 1996.*

Unique Church Guest

 NE SUNNY OCTOBER SABBATH MORNING our church worship had just ended. Members mingled about conversing with one another, when I saw him. He stood five feet nine inches tall, with ruddy complexion and graying hair. He wore a red, plaid, flannel shirt, gray jacket with tan pants. Beside one of our members, he shuffled toward me with an "I need" expression on his face.

"Apparently this man asked several people in the church for money or food, Helen," our member told me. "He could use some help. We told him you were a social worker and could help him."

Immediately, I felt put upon and said to myself, "Any of you people could have helped him." Feeling irritated, I asked the man, "What may I do for you?"

"I'm hungry and need something to eat," he replied.

"I can't give you any money," I told him. "But I'll take you out to lunch."

"I don't care if you can't give me money. I'm just hungry," he said.

"Just wait here," I told him. "I have a couple more people to talk to before we leave." Since I live alone, no way was I going to take this stranger "home" to have lunch with me.

"I'll wait for you," he nodded.

My friend Pat touched my arm and whispered, "What does the little old man want?"

"He told me he's hungry and I plan to take him out to lunch."

"Oh," she said and pressed a ten-dollar bill into my hand. "Let me give you something to help with the food cost."

Fifteen minutes later, after I had wrapped up my conversations with the people I had to see, we walked toward my car. I asked my guest, "What do you have in mind for lunch?"

"Well," he said, "There's a restaurant over on Broadway that has the best soup. It's called, The Great Earth."

Still feeling agitated because this stranger was pawned off on me, I said, "Great Earth! What's the matter with Jack in the Box or Burger King?"

"Well, I just wanted some soup," he persisted.

Once inside my car, I told him, "I don't believe in giving money to strangers because they just go and buy drugs, alcohol, or cigarettes with it." His rosy cheeks made me assume he was a drunkard.

"Oh," he said, "but I don't drink, smoke or use drugs! I'm just hungry."

I said to myself, *Oh, yeah! Right, Mr. Good Guy!*

"What's your name and why are you out here begging then?"

"I know God doesn't want us begging in the street, but I've had some misfortune because I strayed from my mother's instructions. I used to go to church with my mother all the time. But when I left home, I strayed from her Bible teachings."

"Where's home for you?" I asked.

He ignored my question and rambled on, "I know it's wrong to drink and misuse your body and I've never done that."

I said, "You know God continues to watch over all of us even when we go astray."

"I know that. My mother taught me that too."

"How did you happen to come to our church this morning?"

"Lately, I'd been thinking more and more about my youth and upbringing in the church."

"Maybe the Holy Spirit led you to church today," I said.

With a twinkle in his eye, he looked at me. "I know how the Holy Spirit works!"

I drove into The Great Earth's parking lot and stopped. As we strolled toward the restaurant, I said, "You still haven't told me your name or where you live!"

"My name is George Swift and I live at the YMCA. That's where I get my Social Security check."

Once inside the restaurant, I told him, "Order whatever you want to eat." He ordered soup, orange juice and a tuna fish sandwich. As he ate his food and I munched my salad, he continued to say wonderful, marvelous things about God. He always spoke to me with continuous eye contact.

"I'm alive today because of God's unfailing love for me," he said.

I tried to steer our conversation back to his family and his present situation, but he repeatedly put God back into the conversation. He said, "My mother used to say to me, 'When things seem out of the ordinary, that's when God's Spirit is at work.'" He finished his soup and sandwich and put down his spoon, "That was good soup!"

"Have another bowl, if you'd like," I offered.

"You won't mind?"

"No, of course not!" He ordered another bowl of soup. When he finished, I asked him, "Do you want anything more?"

"No, thank you!"

"May I give you a ride to the YMCA?"

"No, thank you," he said as we walked to the car near 3:00 P.M. The parking lot was empty except for my car.

I turned to unlock the car door and said, "George, it's no trouble. It's not far, and I'll be glad to take you to the Y . . ." I never finished my words because when I looked up he was gone! There were no nearby buildings he could have ducked behind to hide from me.

I called, "George, George! Where did you go?" I quickly slipped into my car and drove around the block several times looking for the little old man who was so anxious to talk about our wonderful, marvelous, majestic God, while I was caught up in the mundane things of this world. I could not find him and never saw him again.

As I drove home, I thought about how one-sided our conversation had been. He was willing and ready to glorify God and I was thinking this was another one of his tricks. Often, I regret my actions that day. Here I had a great opportunity to magnify and glorify the name of God by witnessing about His almighty love, mercy and grace—and I fell short! Way too short!

This experience taught me a lesson. I don't treat any stranger in an ordinary fashion any more. I missed so much that day because I was too involved with my own irritations and self.

We're told in Hebrews 13:2, "Be not forgetful to entertain strangers: for thereby some have entertained angels unawares."

As told by Helen Moore.

CHAPTER 3 5

Heartbreak Ridge

ON'S AMBULANCE DODGED SHARPLY around a shell hole on the
dusty road just a few miles from Heartbreak Ridge. Clouds of
gray whirled through his open window. He gasped. Like his dust-
filled nose and throat, his mind choked with troubled thoughts.
He sped away from the danger zone.

"Take it easy, buddy. I hurt." The voice of a wounded soldier on a stretcher
behind him trailed into weakness.

"We'll be at the aid station soon," Ron said over his shoulder.

"Hurry, hurry—oh, the pain!"

Ron's foot pushed harder on the gas pedal, only to release it at the next
sharp mountain curve. "Soon we'll be in the valley. Then I'll step on it," Ron
reassured the bleeding man.

The ambulance bounced over a wooden bridge and roared past a farmer
trudging behind lazy oxen plowing a rice paddy. Around the next bend, Ron
just missed a Korean mother and her black-haired baby strapped to her back
as she crossed the road toward the river embankment to join her friends
pounding laundry with sticks on flat, wet rocks. As he raced through a village

of stone-walled houses thatched with rice straw, he recalled how the night before these same homes stood silvery in the moonlight, snuggled against the ground, with roofs of rice thatch held down securely with crisscrossed ropes like warm fur caps. The ambulance rumbled between gray stone fences guarding sweet potato fields, then through a grove of pink-flowering plum trees and more plowing oxen. Ron smelled the mixture of sweet plum and ox dung through his open window.

Moans from the wounded urged more speed. He accelerated through the bombed town of Yanggu. Only one large building remained, its doors, windows, and roof blown away. Then up the last steep incline and down the narrow, sharp grade. Ron's eyes, gritty with sand, searched to see around each rocky bend.

"At last! We're at the aid station." Ron's clammy palms released the steering wheel. He hopped out, opened the back of the ambulance, and grabbed a stretcher.

"Here, let me give you a hand." Ted, the aid-station medic slapped Ron's shoulder. "You made it again, old buddy." They lowered the stretcher and wheeled it inside.

"Did you see the new list of names posted at the major's office, Ted? Mine's on it. Guess my next assignment will be on the front lines at Heartbreak Ridge."

"Did you see my name on that list, Ron?" Ted asked as they carried the last wounded soldier into the station.

"No, didn't see it."

Ted followed Ron to the ambulance. "I'd like a change and more challenge. This aid station gets boring." Ted stood back as Ron started the ambulance and headed for the front once again, gravel pelting the metal sides of his truck.

Ron had been driving the ambulance for only several weeks when the major decided there were too many C.O.s (conscientious objectors) at stations two and three. And that was when the list of names assigned to frontline duty had been posted.

After the next ambulance run, Ron used his break to reread the posted list. Yes, he had read correctly. His name was plainly on that list. It had not mysteriously disappeared.

Ron had come to Korea willingly to aid his country in the fight for human rights, but unlike any other, this particular assignment haunted him. It left him with a strange feeling, a hunch he would never return to the United States and home.

Finally in the dark, cold night he slipped away. Under a dwarf pine he prayed, "Dear God, deliver me from this assignment or protect me through it all. Thy will be done." He remained on his knees and pled with God until the fear left him and peace filled his heart.

The next day he checked the list again. He blinked. A line had been drawn through his name. And at the bottom a new name had been added: Ted's. Ted had taken his place on the front lines.

A few months later Ron, by then in mechanics' school learning ambulance repair, heard that Ted had taken a fatal wound on Heartbreak Ridge. Ted, the buddy who had led their Sabbath gatherings' song service with such talent and enthusiasm; Ted the selfless; Ted, who had taken Ron's place.

And thirty years later, Ted was still the one who best reminded Ron of Another who had chosen front-line duty, and on a heartbreaking ridge called Golgotha had died. "Greater love hath no man than this, that a man lay down his life for his friends."

As told by Myron Baybarz.
Published by Insight, *April 5, 1983.*

A Chinese Elijah

ELIJAH WAS NOT THE ONLY ONE whom God has fed by means of ravens—as demonstrated by the following story told by Mrs. Howard Taylor of the China Inland Mission.

Li was an elderly man when he became a Christian in the late 1800s. Ministering to the needs of others, he lived a simple life, relying day by day on the Lord and often experiencing hard times. His resources were few, and even these were often stretched to their utmost.

Nearby, in a large temple, lived a cousin who was the priest in charge. He would come to see his relative, Li, from time to time, bringing with him a little present of bread or grain from his ample supply. Old Li would always say, "T'ien Fu tih en tien!" meaning "My heavenly Father's grace!" Thus he indicated his faith in the kindness and care of God. But the priest did not see it that way at all.

"Where does your heavenly Father's grace come in, I should like to know," he would remonstrate. "The grain is mine. I bring it to you. And if I didn't, you would soon starve for all that your God would care. He has nothing to do with it at all!"

"But it is my heavenly Father Who puts it into your heart to care for me," old Li would answer.

"That is all very well, cousin. But we shall see what will happen if I bring the grain no more." And for a week or two he kept away. He felt badly because in his heart he esteemed the old man for the works of mercy in which he was constantly engaged.

Meanwhile, old Li's supplies dwindled even further. At last the day came when he had nothing left for another meal. He had not a single coin to buy a morsel of bread. Kneeling along in his room, he poured out his heart to God in prayer. He knew very well that his Father in heaven would not, could not, forget him. After pleading for God's blessing on his work and upon the people in his neighborhood, he reminded the Lord of what the priest had said. He asked that God would send him that day his daily bread in order to honor His own name before his cousin the priest.

The answer was not long in coming. Then and there, while still kneeling in prayer, the old man heard a clamor outside his window. There was a flapping of wings in the courtyard outside and the sound of something falling to the ground. He rose and went to the door. A number of ravens, which are quite common in that part of China, were flying about in great commotion. As he looked up, a large piece of meat fell at his very feet! One of the birds, chased by the others, had dropped it just at that moment on that spot! In the Orient, it's true that one becomes accustomed to the sight of flocks of crows hovering over the market place, watching for a chance to seize a piece of meat from a butcher's stall.

Thankfully, the old man picked up the unexpected portion, saying, "My heavenly Father's kindness!" Then he looked about him to see what had fallen before he came outside. He soon discovered a large piece of bread, all cooked and ready to eat. Another bird had dropped that also, and here was his dinner bountifully provided from the heavens!

With a heart overflowing with joy, the old man kindled a fire and began to cook the meat. While the pot was still boiling, the door opened, and in walked his cousin the priest.

"Look," Li said, smiling as he pointed to the pot simmering over the fire.

For a long while the priest would not lift the lid, certain that there was nothing inside but water boiling. At length, however, the savory odor was not to be mistaken, and overcome by curiosity, he looked inside the earthen pot. He was astonished to see the excellent dinner inside. "Where did you get this?" he cried.

My heavenly Father sent it," Li answered happily. "He put it into your heart, you know, to bring me a little grain from time to time. But when you would do so no longer, it was quite easy for Him to find another messenger." And he sat down and told his cousin the whole incident of his prayer and the coming of the ravens.

The priest was much impressed by what he saw and heard. It proved to be the beginning of a great change in his life. For from that time, he began to seriously consider the claims of Christianity. He became, in time, an earnest inquirer and eventually confessed his faith in Christ and the heavenly Father. He gave up his comfortable living in the temple for the joy of the gospel that now satisfied his soul. He supported himself as a teacher and became a much-respected deacon in the church. During the troubles of the Boxer Rebellion in 1900, he endured terrible tortures and finally gave his life for his faith in Jesus.

CHAPTER 37

A Voice in the Night

ASTOR JOSEPH STENNETT WAS WORRIED when Caleb, one of his parishioners, failed to appear for services. The winter of 1801–1802 was particularly severe in Wales, and the pastor feared that the poor collier and his family might be snowed in and in need. However, the following week, Caleb and his family were able to make their way to the church in spite of the deep snow. When Pastor Stennett inquired about their well-being, Caleb reported that the Lord had provided for them in the following way.

One night during the previous week, the family had eaten the last of the food in their simple home. Not a morsel was left for the morning, and there seemed no human possibility of getting anything. But Caleb found his mind was calm and composed. He trusted a God who always provides. The family knelt and prayed, asking God to provide their daily bread. They then retired to rest and slept soundly until the next morning.

Before Caleb had arisen from bed, he heard a knock on the door. He went to see who it was and saw a man unknown to him standing at his door. A horse stood in the road, heavily loaded. The man inquired if this was the

home of Caleb the collier. Upon being answered in the affirmative, he asked
Caleb to help him take the load from the horse.

"What is in the bundles?" Caleb asked.

"Food and provisions," answered the man.

"Who has sent these things?" Caleb wanted to know.

"I believe God must have sent it," was the reply. And try as he might, Caleb
could elicit nothing further from the man.

This was the story Caleb related to his pastor the following week.

A few days later, Pastor Stennett was visiting in the home of Dr. Talbot, a
physician in a nearby town whose wife was a member of his congregation.
Dr. Talbot, himself, was a generous man, but an unbeliever. For the benefit of
the doctor, Pastor Stennett led the conversation around to the matter of God's
providential care in answer to prayer. He mentioned the recent case of the
collier, Caleb. Dr. Talbot smiled knowingly, and when the pastor had
finished, he told him that he had a tale of his own to tell.

Some months before, the doctor had been riding in the hills when he came
upon a religious meeting being held in a barn. He stopped and listened for
about half an hour, watching the speaker and the listeners. He particularly
noticed one man who had a well-thumbed Bible and who was following the
speaker with the deepest interest.

As the meeting broke up and the people began to go their ways, the doctor
found himself riding for a while alongside the man whom he had been
noticing during the service. He learned that the man's name was Caleb. He
was impressed by his intelligence as they talked. However, after they parted,
he had thought no more of this experience or of the man until the winter
came with its storms and great snows.

One night in bed—he couldn't tell for sure whether he was awake or

asleep—he thought he heard a voice saying, "Send provisions to Caleb!"
He was startled, but concluded that it must have been a dream. He tried to
go back to sleep. A few moments later he imagined he heard the same words
again—this time louder and stronger. He awoke his wife and told her what he
had heard. She persuaded him that he must be dreaming, and soon she was
fast asleep again.

Not so her husband. His mind was so impressed with the words he had
heard that he couldn't sleep. He tumbled and tossed about. At last he heard a
voice again. "Get up and send provisions to Caleb!" The voice was so
commanding that he could resist no longer.

He arose and called his servant, telling him to bring around the horse.
He went to his pantry and stuffed two large saddlebags as full as he possibly
could, packing them with whatever he could find. Then he helped the servant
load the horse and told him to take the provisions to Caleb.

"Caleb, sir?" the man inquired. "What Caleb would that be, sir?"

"I know little about him," replied the doctor. "But his name is Caleb. He is
a collier and lives in the hills. Once you are in the area, you should be able to
make inquiries and find the house."

As the doctor concluded his portion of the story, Pastor Stennett rejoiced
to learn how God's providence had once again responded to the prayer of
faith—even if it meant using an unbeliever as the means to do so.

A Welcome Companion

◌

HIS STORY—A REMARKABLE INSTANCE of God's providence through instantaneous answer to prayer—comes from the early days of Methodism.

A minister of the Welsh Calvinistic Methodist Church had need to travel by horseback through a desolate and lonely region in northern Wales. On a particular morning, with the road running for quite a distance between high, thick hedges on either side, he noticed a rough-looking man walking on the other side of the hedge. The man carried a sharp reaping hook and kept pace with the minister, separated from him by the hedge through which there was no passage. However, farther ahead, the minister could see a gate where it would be necessary for him to dismount in order to open it and pass through. It seemed clear to him that the dangerous man on the other side of the hedge intended to intercept him at the gate.

The minister had a bag of money that he had collected for a chapel building, and he felt that not only was the money in danger, but quite possibly his life as well. He stopped his horse in the road and bowed his head to pray for God's special aid and protection. His horse seemed restive, and in any case the minister was not disposed to make his prayer too long. Looking up after a moment of silent prayer, he was surprised to see a man on a white horse standing alongside him in the road. He had heard nothing in the brief moments his eyes were closed in prayer—no sound of a horse approaching! Unable to account for the sudden, yet welcome, appearance of a companion at such a moment, he nevertheless turned and expressed to the horseman his relief at his presence.

The stranger made no reply, but looked steadily at the gate ahead. Following his gaze, the minister saw the man with the reaping hook emerge from his place of concealment and run away across the field to the left. He had evidently seen that the minister was not alone and had abandoned his intended assault.

With the cause for alarm now past, the minister endeavored to enter into conversation with his deliverer, but without the slightest success. Not a word did the stranger give in reply to questions or comments. Nevertheless, the minister continued to talk as they rode toward the gate. He felt somewhat disconcerted at the other's silence, not understanding why he would not speak. At length, he said, "Can there be the slightest doubt that my prayer was heard and that the Lord sent you for my deliverance?" Only then did he hear the stranger speak—and then only a single word.

"Amen!" said the man on the horse.

Although the minister continued his endeavors to engage his companion in conversation, with questions in both English and Welsh, not another word was forthcoming.

They were now approaching the gate, and the minister spurred his horse forward with the purpose of opening it. He did so and waited for the other to pass through. He didn't come. The minister turned his head to see why he waited—and he was gone! Dumfounded, the minister looked back down the road in the direction from which they had just been riding. His companion on the white horse was nowhere to be seen. He had not gone through the gate; he could not have leaped the high hedge which shut in the road on either side. Where could he have disappeared?

"Was it possible," the minister asked himself, "that I had seen no man or horse at all, that it was all but a creation of my imagination?" He tried to convince himself that this must be the explanation, but it was useless. Unless someone had been with him, why had the man with the murderous-looking sickle fled so precipitously? No, the horseman could be no imaginary illusion.

The minister turned these things over and over in his mind, and then a feeling of profound awe began to creep over his soul. He remembered the singular manner in which the horseman had first appeared. He recalled his companion's reluctance to speak, and then the single word which he had uttered and which had come in response to mentioning the name of the Lord and His divine providence. The conviction came to his heart that God had indeed answered his prayer for deliverance by immediately sending one of His angels to protect him! He could believe nothing less.

Dismounting, the minister threw himself on his knees at the side of the road and offered up a prayer of thanksgiving to the God who had so clearly rescued him from danger.

To the end of his life, the minister had no doubt that his companion on the white horse was one of God's angels sent for his deliverance in answer to his prayer for protection.

Christian Herald (London)

CHAPTER 39

Across the Raging River

N THE EARLY DAYS OF CHRISTIAN WORK at the Spion Kop Zulu Mission in Africa, Brother and Sister Lange worked among the Kafir people. Their daughter, Mrs. Blaine, told the following story of divine deliverance at a time when there was unrest throughout the region. "Nothing will ever convince me," said her mother, "that God did not send angels to deliver us in that night of peril."

"For some days the Kafirs had been sharpening their 'assagais,' which was a sign of an impending raid. Mother could speak Kafir like a native and knew of the trouble that was brewing. Friendly Kafirs warned Father and Mother to flee, for they could not protect them from the raiders, they said. At length as the warnings became more urgent, an invitation arrived from a friendly chief beyond the river offering refuge to the missionaries. Mother and Father started by ox cart for the chief's kraal. They had hardly begun their journey when the uprising broke across the land, pitting tribe against tribe. Mother and Father had to push on for their lives with all the speed that could be urged from the slow-moving oxen.

"'Where are you going,' asked friendly Kafirs whom they met.

"'We're going to Umdushani's kraal,' Mother answered. Since she spoke Kafir well, she most often did the talking.

"'You will never get there,' came the reply. 'The Kafirs will kill you.'

"But Mother and Father pressed on toward the river. There they found that the river was in flood stage with the water coming down in a torrent. The steep banks were full to the brim. Their native guides said that it was no use, they could never get across. It was raining, and night was fast coming on. In front of them was the swollen river, and daylight the next morning was sure to bring down the hostile Kafirs upon them.

"Mother had taken ill and could not be moved from the wagon. There they were in the rain and gathering darkness with the warring Kafirs behind them. Before them the raging river closed the way of escape. The native guides were in terror, and the oxen were almost unmanageable. Mother and Father could only lift their hearts to God in prayer for help.

"Just then two black men came up to them out of the rain. In calm, forceful voices they said, 'Do you want to cross the river?'

"'Yes,' replied Mother. 'We must sleep tonight at Umdushani's kraal. But the river is so full we cannot cross.'

"'We will take you over,' said the men.

"They asked Mother and Father to sit perfectly still in the cart. The men took charge, quieting the frightened oxen and guiding them into the river. Slowly they moved out into the swift-flowing water, continuing to keep the animals moving until they scrambled safely out upon the banks of the other side. Those who watched the little party make the perilous crossing were amazed. When the wagon stopped on the other side, Mother and Father wanted to thank the two men for what they had done. But they were gone! They had disappeared as suddenly as they had appeared at the critical moment. The native guides had never seen the two men before. They did not know where they came from, nor did they see them as they withdrew.

"It had all been so sudden, so quiet and providential, that Mother and Father could see in it only the direct hand of God bringing deliverance as they called upon Him for help. They soon reached the safety of Umdushani's kraal and placed themselves under his protection for the duration of the trouble.

"Often, Mother and Father said that they believed the angels of God were sent to them that evening beside the raging river to deliver them.

CHAPTER 40

Angels on Guard

HIS AMAZING STORY OF ANGEL PROTECTION in the mid-nineteenth century comes from Sumatra. A man by the name of Von Asselt was the first European missionary to gain a foothold in bringing the gospel to the wild Battak people of this large Indonesian island just south of the Malay Peninsula. Here is Von Asselt's account of miraculous intervention by angels to preserve his life:

It is difficult for anyone who has not experienced it to understand what it means to stand alone in a strange place among a warlike people, unable to make myself understood, and not understanding a single word of the local language—but understanding all too well the suspicious looks and hostile gestures. The first two years I spent among the Battaks were so difficult that I shudder even now when I think of them. The first year I was all alone; the second, my wife had joined me at our lonely post.

Often it seems that we were surrounded not only by hostile men, but by the hostile powers of darkness. Often an inexplicable, unutterable fear would come over us so that we would get up in the middle of the night and go to our knees to pray or read the Word of God in order to find relief.

After having lived in that place for two years, we moved to a spot several hours inland among a tribe of people who received us more kindly. We built a small house there—three rooms—and life became somewhat easier and more cheerful.

After we had been in this new situation for a few months, I was sitting on a bench in front of the house, when a man appeared from the district where we had lived earlier. I knew him from our time there. He sat down beside me on the bench and began to talk for a while of this and that. Finally, he said, "*Tuan* [teacher], I have a request."

"Yes. What is it?"

"I would like to have a look at your watchmen close at hand."

"What watchmen do you mean? I don't have any watchmen."

"I'm talking about the watchmen you station around your house at night to protect you."

"But I have no watchmen," I insisted. "I have only a little boy who herds the animals and a cook. They would make poor watchmen."

The man looked at me unbelievingly as if to say, "Don't try to fool me, for I know better!"

Then he asked, "May I look through your house to see if they are hiding there?"

"Of course," I replied. "Look through it. You won't find anybody."

So he searched every corner, even going through the beds, but he came out again much disappointed. Then I began to question him a bit. I asked him to tell me why he thought I had watchmen.

He seemed reluctant to answer, but at last he replied, "When you first came to us, *tuan*, we were very angry at you. We didn't want you living among us. We didn't trust you. So we came together and decided to kill you and your wife. We came to your house night after night. But whenever we came near, we always saw a double row of watchmen standing close together all around your house. They held shining weapons. We were afraid to attack them to get into your house.

"So we went to an assassin [at that time there was a special guild of men among the Battaks who would kill anyone for hire]. We asked him to kill you and your wife. We explained about the watchmen. He laughed at us and called us cowards. He said, 'I fear no God or devil. I will get through these watchmen easily.'

"We all came together that evening and followed the assassin as he went down the path toward your house, swinging his weapon around his head. As we neared your house, we hung back and allowed him to go forward alone. A short time later, he came running back down the path. He told us, 'I don't dare risk trying to get through! There are two rows of big, strong men standing there, shoulder to shoulder, and their weapons shine like fire!'

"Now, tell me, *tuan*, who are these watchmen? Haven't you seen them?"

"No," I replied. "I have never seen them."

"And your wife—hasn't she seen them?"

"No, my wife has never seen them either."

"But *we* have all seen them. How is that?"

Then I went into the house and brought out my Bible. Holding it open before him, I said, "See. This book is the Word of God. In it He promises to guard and defend us. We believe that Word, so we don't need to see the watchmen. But you do not believe. So God has to show you the watchmen in order to help you believe."

First published in Sontags-blatt furs Haus.

Dancing for Rain

ANNY GUINNESS TELLS OF A TIME of threatened famine in the
African Congo many years ago when missionaries were first
bringing the gospel to that land. The rainy season was passing
rapidly, but there was no rain. One evening the missionary heard
an unusual sound—a drum beating in the villages, but with a different tempo
and cadence than he had heard before.

He asked one of the boys nearby what the drum signified, and the boy said
that the drum was beating to assemble the people to dance that night for rain.

"But you know that dancing will not bring rain, don't you?" asked the
missionary.

"Oh, yes, teacher, it will," the young boy assured him.

"Nonsense! How can beating a drum and dancing make the rain fall?
If God wants it to rain, it will, but not otherwise."

"Ah, well, teacher, you will see. Just notice now if it doesn't rain before
tomorrow morning!"

The missionary was discouraged. Even the students at the mission school
were under the spell of the local superstitions. "Oh, Lord," he prayed, "forbid
that Your rain should fall in apparent response to the invocations of the drum."

The night passed without rain. Many succeeding nights passed, and still no rain fell. Suspicion grew in the minds of the people that the foreign missionary was driving away the rain god. What the missionary had said to the boy at the mission school came to the ears of the chieftain who sent for the missionary and told him that the people believed he was the one responsible for withholding the rain.

"It is not I who is preventing the rain," replied the missionary. "It is your people."

"How is that?" the chieftain demanded.

"It is like this. God owns all the clouds, for He made them. Season by season, He has sent the rain to you unasked, and you have had plenty to eat in your villages. But who among you has ever once thanked *Him?* Instead, you have praised and thanked your rain gods."

"What, then, should we do?" the chieftain wanted to know.

This was a good question. What answer should the missionary give? There seemed to be but one answer, and that was to take up the challenge of the chief in the name of God.

"Appoint a day for all the people to gather," the missionary replied, "and ask God to give them rain. If they will come to Him with sincere hearts and put away their rain gods, He will listen."

"Your words are good," declared the chief. "I appoint tomorrow as the day!"

The next day the people flocked in large numbers to the little mission church and filled it to overflowing. Leaders and people from all the surrounding villages were present. After the missionary had spoken to the people for a while, he offered a prayer to God, pleading with Him to vindicate His name and send the desperately-needed rain. After the prayer, the people dispersed and returned to their villages.

All the rest of that day, the missionary and his fellow workers on the compound agonized in prayer to God. And toward evening, the answer to their prayer seemed to be at hand. Thick, black clouds rolled overhead. But alas, they shifted and broke apart and disappeared!

It was a difficult trial of their faith, but still they continued praying that God would send rain and demonstrate His power over the heavens. Through the night they watched and prayed. Before dawn, the clouds came overhead once more. This time they did not disperse until a glorious, refreshing shower had fallen upon the thirsty land.

Not all the villagers accepted the rain as evidence of the power of the missionary's God. But many were convicted and turned to Him. And to the missionaries, in their isolation and helplessness against the powers of darkness, the rain was unmistakable evidence that God had heard their prayers and sent them a sign that He was ever with them to help and to deliver.

On the Congo

CHAPTER 4 2

Help in Time of Need

R. P. A. DE FOREST, for many years superintendent of the Lake
Geneva Sanitarium in Switzerland, has told of how God
miraculously provided for his needs during his student days. His
purpose in doing so, he said, was to give glory to God and to
encourage young Christians.

"In 1893, I was a medical student in Cincinnati, Ohio. I started my studies
with no financial resources beyond what I could earn as a nurse. But I had
promised God that if he would help me get through medical school I would
dedicate my life to Him as a missionary doctor. And he provided work for
me, but times were difficult financially, and on one occasion my faith was
especially put to the test.

"I had a wife and two small children. In spite of working as hard as I could,
I could not earn quite enough to support them adequately and pay all my fees
and expenses at the university. A time came when our clothing began to give
out. This situation was brought keenly to my attention when my wife was
obliged, at last, to stay home from worship services because she had no shoes
fit to wear in public.

"Naturally, I felt very badly at this state of affairs. But had we not had proof after proof of God's tender care and guiding hand? Following prayer to Him who hears in secret, we lay down and slept that night feeling assured that God would provide in some way for our great need.

"That night I dreamed that a person came to me and said, 'If you go to the house of Sister _____ in Winton Place, you will find the help you need.' The next morning, I related this extraordinary incident to my wife. And although I could not quite believe that the dream was different from any other dream, I resolved to go the following weekend and visit the lady mentioned in my dream. My small faith was amply rewarded, as will be seen.

"I arrived at the home of Sister _____ and found her enjoying a visit from her brother. I talked with them about my medical studies, my desire to prepare myself for mission service, and my family—but I purposely avoided any intimation of want in order that I might know for a certainty if the Lord had sent the dream.

"The brother of Sister _____ left the room before I did, but without bidding me goodbye. I soon rose from my chair as well, and left the house to return home, saying to myself that, after all, my dream was like all other dreams—nothing more. I was outside the gate when a servant came running after me and asked me to come back inside, saying that the brother wished to see me.

"I returned, wondering what would happen. The gentleman led me into a room and showed me a heap of clothing that he had selected for me—just what I needed to replenish my depleted wardrobe. I stammered out my thanks, but still I kept thinking of my wife's lack of shoes. After satisfying himself that the clothing would fit me, my benefactor reached into his pocket and laid five dollars upon the pile of clothing, saying, 'I was impressed to help you because you said you wanted to be a missionary, and it has been my practice for several years to help young men who desire to serve the Lord.'

Then he added as he handed me the money, 'This will not come amiss, I presume.'

"You can imagine my feelings. I hurried home with a heart filled with praise to God and particularly thankful that He had not withheld His mercies on account of my meager faith. When I got home, my wife and I rejoiced at the good measure God had given. Then and there we took courage that He would never leave us or forsake us. Nor has He in all the years since then.

CHAPTER 4 3

Poisoned in Tibet

MONG THE PIONEER MISSIONARIES in Tibet was a young English woman, Miss Annie Taylor. With a burden on her heart for this country, she lived among Tibetans on the Indian side of the border until she learned the language. Then in 1890 she crossed the frontier in spite of regulations against her entry—a young woman, alone, taking her stand on the forbidden ground because of the gospel commission: "Go ye into all the world."

The Tibetan authorities ordered her to leave. The captain of the guard for the Dong-Kya Pass traveled from the fort at Khamba-jong to settle what should be done regarding her. Eventually, she was moved to Tumlong and allowed to live in a room of the monastery there. But the local people were instructed not to sell her any food, and she found it extremely difficult to live. On one occasion she followed a caravan over the stony roads in order to pick up the grains of parched corn that were falling from a small hole in one of the mule packs.

Not all the local people were hostile to the English woman. Occasionally women would surreptitiously allow grain to fall in the roadway for her. Like the birds of the air, Miss Taylor would pick it up, thanking God for the timely provision. She held on to her desire to win souls over to Christ in Tibet and refused to be driven out.

Most of the villagers resented her living in their midst, and attempted to discourage her and force her to leave. They would ask her frequently what they were to do with her body if she died. She replied that she was not going to die just then, but would live and continue to talk to them about Jesus. The villagers, however, had other plans for the young woman. In those days, the Tibetan people had a custom of "praying people dead." They began the process for the young missionary. At the same time, they determined to help their prayers along in a most effective manner by poisoning her.

One day the wife of the most important man in the village invited Miss Taylor to eat. She prepared a dish of rice and eggs. As she was eating, Miss Taylor's suspicions were aroused by some stray conversation; she began to suspect that the eggs she had eaten were poisoned. Sure enough, shortly after eating, she became violently ill with all the symptoms of acute poisoning.

She felt her strength ebbing; her heart was beating erratically. Her head was spinning on the verge of unconsciousness. She looked up and saw a crowd of villagers gathering silently about her. She knew then that she had been poisoned by deliberate and deadly design and that the people were gathering in curiosity to see her die.

There she was—a young woman all alone in Tibet. Yet she was not truly alone. The One who had promised, "Lo, I am with you always" still remained by her side. His angels were present, and His Spirit at that moment brought to her memory the promise, "If they drink any deadly thing, it shall not hurt them." The conviction came to her mind that God would save her. With her strength fast disappearing, she laid hold of God's promise and asked him to honor it just then—not for her sake alone, but for the sake of the Tibetan villagers.

Immediately, she felt the blood once more tingling in her veins. Her heart began to beat normally; her strength returned. She got up in the strength of the Lord, and to the great amazement of those who had come to witness her last moments, she took out a portion of the Scriptures in Tibetan and began to talk to them of Jesus and His power to save them in spite of their attempt to take her life.

In later years, she said little publicly about this dramatic deliverance from God's hand. Yet there was no doubt in her mind that God had interposed in a miraculous way to save her from death by poison.

The Missionary Review

CHAPTER 44

Rescue at Sea

WHEN HELEN STEINHAUER WAS A CHILD, she lived in Jamaica where her parents were Moravian missionaries. When the parents' health began to fail, they decided they must leave Jamaica. Taking passage on a sailing ship bound for New Orleans, the father, mother, and daughter began their journey—little anticipating what lay ahead. The ship was driven far from its course by a storm. Following the storm, a dead calm settled upon the ocean. The ship carried provisions only for a few days and it became necessary to ration food and water.

What happened in the terrible days that followed is told by Helen in a story that appeared in the November 8, 1894, issue of *Youth's Instructor.*

"As the days lengthened into weeks, our sufferings were extreme. I remember gnawing at a kid glove for what nutriment it might contain. We were put upon rations of half a ship biscuit and half a pint of water in the twenty-four hours—a very small allowance of food, and a still smaller one of drink beneath a semi-tropical sun. . .

"Some gulped their portion of water as soon as it was given them. Others hugged it to them with fierce eagerness, as long as they could, dreading lest a stronger hand might snatch it away. At length our tongues became so swollen from protracted thirst that we could scarcely close our mouths. My mother found that dipping cloths into the sea and binding them dripping wet about our throats afforded some relief, but oh how maddening it was to see water, water everywhere, yet not a drop to drink! Our sufferings from hunger were extreme, but the suffering from thirst was great beyond expression.

"When four weeks had nearly dragged their slow length along, it was decided that to make our scant allowance last one day longer, some of our number were to be thrown overboard. The lot was to be cast at night, but the result was not to be made known until just before the food was given out, in the hope that deliverance might come before the measure was put into execution.

"My father and a Spanish gentleman slept on deck, but my mother and I, being the only females on board, besides the captains' wife and three women in the hold, retired to our berths in the cabin.

"Of course many and importunate prayers had been offered all along, but my mother determined to spend the entire night in supplication, which she accordingly did. At early daylight she sank into the sleep of exhaustion, from which she was awakened by my father's voice saying, 'My dear, we think we see a ship!'

"'Oh,' exclaimed my mother wearily, 'it will pass us by like all the rest.' We had been frequently tantalized by the sight of steamers passing like dim specks on the western horizon, but so far away that we could not hail them, nor could they see our signals of distress. Then recollecting her night's occupation, mother repentantly added, 'No, God forgive me! It is an answer to my prayer. It will come to our relief.'

"'Don't be too sure, wife,' said my father gently. 'I would not have you disappointed. If it be God's will for us, it will come to our relief.'

"'It is His will,' replied my mother confidently. 'I am sure that help is at hand.'

"As quickly as possible we dressed and crawled up the narrow hatchway. I shall never forget the sight that presented itself as we got on deck. There, on the side of the vessel nearest the object from which the hoped-for relief was to come, were gathered the entire ship's company. Not a word was spoken, but as the naked eye could not yet discern anything, in breathless silence the ship's spyglass was passed from one to the other, that each might see.

"It certainly seemed as if it were a vessel. Yes, now we were quite sure of the fact. But would it come our way? Or must we again see it vanish out of sight like the ship of a dream?

"No! It came nearer and nearer and nearer still. Soon we could see it without the aid of the spyglass. Signals we could not make, we were far too weak and helpless. But it came on, nevertheless, straight and true, directly bearing down upon us. By and by the ship hailed us. 'Ship ahoy!'

"But not a man on board had strength of voice to make reply.

"Still it came on nearer, nor did it stop until within easy distance of our luckless vessel. A boat was let down, into which stepped four men, one of whom was evidently the captain. The supreme tension of that moment is indelibly impressed upon my mind, child though I was at the time.

"The captain was the first to board us, and as he set foot on our deck and saw our wretched plight, he lifted his hat and said solemnly, 'Now I believe that there is a God in heaven!'

"Our rescuers proved to be from one of the small steamers that tow sailing vessels into harbor across the bar. By the rules that then bound them (they may be changed now, I cannot say), they were not allowed to go beyond a certain distance from port to look for vessels needing their assistance. But the captain proceeded to unfold a strange story.

"After he had gone the full limit from port allowed, he felt unaccountably impelled to go still farther, although there was not a vessel in sight. His mate remonstrated with him, reminding him of the fine to which he laid himself liable if he persisted.

"'I can't help it. I've got to go on!' was his only reply.

"After a while he became desperately seasick, a thing that had not happened to him before in twenty years. He was compelled to take to his berth, yet he refused to turn back, but bade the crew to push still farther out to sea. Then the crew mutinied, for they were growing short of provisions themselves. They determined to take things into their own hands, thinking that the captain must have lost his senses.

"At this, his distress of mind became agonizing, and he implored them to go on. He promised them that if they saw nothing by sunrise the next morning to justify his action, he would give up and promptly put back to port.

"The men consented reluctantly, and when day dawned the man at the masthead reported a black, motionless object far out to sea.

"'Make for it!' exclaimed the captain emphatically. 'That's what we've come after.'

"At this instant his seasickness left him, and he took command as before. On reaching us and seeing our emaciated forms and general wretchedness, the conviction forced itself upon him with overwhelming power that he had been supernaturally guided, and that there *was* a God in heaven—something he had not believed for years. Later, when he learned how my feeble mother had spent the entire night in prayer, he broadened his view to include that fact that the God who had guided him was a prayer-hearing and a prayer-answering God as well.

"Thus it was that exactly four weeks from the day we left Kingston, Jamaica, we arrived in New Orleans."

CHAPTER 45

Turning an Enemy's Heart

HIS AMAZING STORY happened in the early 1800s in New England, but its message of God's personal care is as current as tomorrow.

An upright man, Deacon P., was financially ruined by endorsing the note of a man whom he trusted. With a wife sick to death and a little girl, he was forced to seek other employment in midwinter. One morning when his resources were gone and no work had been found, his little girl reported that the wood and the candles were all used up. "How shall we take care of mother tonight?" she asked her father.

He fled to his room, and in an agony of prayer he poured out his heart there, beseeching the Lord for help. Forgetting all other needs, he pled again and again for the two articles he especially needed, repeating his prayer earnestly. At last, he arose from his knees in assurance that his prayer had been heard and with a calm heart. He left home expecting deliverance, looking for it, but in one way only—through his own earnings. He must find work!

But after a fruitless day of seeking employment, he returned home filled with gloom. As he entered the gate, he was startled to see before him a generous supply of wood. His little daughter opened the door and exclaimed, "Father, we have some wood and some candles!"

"Where did you get them? Are you sure they were not left here by mistake?"

"Oh, no, father. They were not left by mistake. A man knocked at the door with his whip, and when I opened it, he asked if you lived here. I told him you did. Then he said, 'Here are some candles and a load of wood for him.' I asked him if you had sent him, and he replied, 'I rather guess your father doesn't know anything about it.'

"'Then who did send them?' I asked.

"'Oh,' he said, 'I mustn't tell. But you may say to your father that they are a present.'"

To whom they were indebted for the relief was a mystery. And it particularly amazed Deacon P. that the very things needed—candles and wood—should be sent and nothing else. He was sure he had not mentioned his need of these particular articles to any human ear. He questioned his daughter anew. She described the man who had knocked at the door and the wagon he drove and the team of horses. A new thought struck Deacon P. "Why," he said to himself, "that team belongs to my old enemy, Mr. Graff. Can it be possible that he is the donor? If so, surely the finger of God has touched his heart."

He was so convinced that their benefactor could be no other person that he resolved to call on that gentleman immediately. The two men had been friends, but something had come between them in that past that had earned Deacon P. the inveterate enmity of Mr. Graff. Try as the deacon might to conciliate the man and to show him that there was no hostility on his part, his former friend refused to acknowledge his attempts to end the quarrel. This was the man to whom Deacon P. now made his way.

He entered Mr. Graff's place of business. For the first time in years, its proprietor looked up with a nod of recognition. It was evident that something had softened his heart.

"I have called," said the deacon, "to ask if you can tell me who sent some wood and candles to my house today."

"Yes. I sent them."

"You are very kind. But how did you come to do so?"

"Let me first ask if you truly needed them."

"I cannot express to you how much."

"Well, then, I suppose I must explain," said Mr. Graff. "It is all very strange. This morning, about ten o'clock, I was busy at my work, when suddenly I seemed to hear a voice that said, 'Send some wood to Deacon P. He is in want.' I was astonished. I tried to put the thought from my mind, and went to work more earnestly. I couldn't believe you needed help. And I, of all people, couldn't send it to you. But the voice said again, clearly, distinctly, 'Send some wood to Deacon P. He is in want!' I tried to dismiss the idea as a silly fantasy of my brain. But it was no use. I had to follow it. The more I fought against it, the more vivid and irresistible was the impression. At last in order to find peace—and in some awe—I told my clerk to load the wagon with wood and leave it at your door.

"For a moment I was at peace. But only for a moment. The imperative whisper came again, 'Send some candles, too!'

"'This is absurd!' I said to myself. 'I won't gratify this whim.' But again I was so beset by the mandate and so distressed, that I handed my clerk a package of candles also as a means of relieving my torment.

"This matter has been in my mind ever since. Sometimes I have thought it was a peculiar impulse of my own mind. And then again, the strange character of the impression—so unexpected, so solemn and powerful—and the singular peace which followed compliance with its demands has made me almost believe it must have been of supernatural origin."

"It is, indeed, the work of God who is wonderful in all His dealings with us," replied Deacon P. "It was about ten o'clock this morning, I well remember, that I pled with God in an agony of prayer I never before experienced, for the very articles you sent me. It was then, too, that my prayer was heard, and I was filled with the conviction that relief would come."

From the New England Reflector.

A Note from the Editors